PENNSYLVANIA ODDITIES

VOLUME 2

MARLIN BRESSI

SUNBURY PRESS

Mechanicsburg, PA USA

Published by Sunbury Press, Inc.
Mechanicsburg, Pennsylvania

SUNBURY
PRESS
www.sunburypress.com

For information about special discounts for bulk purchases, please contact Sunbury Press
Orders Dept. at (855) 338-8359 or orders@sunburypress.com.

To request one of our authors for speaking engagements or book signings, please contact
Sunbury Press Publicity Dept. at publicity@sunburypress.com.

FIRST SUNBURY PRESS EDITION: June 2020

Set in Adobe Garamond | Interior design by Crystal Devine | Cover design by Lawrence
Knorr | Edited by Lawrence Knorr

Publisher's Cataloging-in-Publication Data
Names: Bress, Marlin, author.
Title: Pennsylvania oddities volume 2 / Marlin Bressi.
Description: First trade paperback edition. | Mechanicsburg, PA : Sunbury Press, 2020.
Summary: Author Marlin Bressi has compiled bizarre stories that happened in Pennsylvania
that are so strange, they have to be true. All accounts are based on historical newspaper
reports.
Identifiers: ISBN : 978-1-620063-89-7 (softcover).
Subjects: History / US History / Mid-Atlantic | TRUE CRIME / Historical.

Product of the United States of America
0 1 1 2 3 5 8 13 21 34 55

Continue the Enlightenment!

CONTENTS

INTRODUCTION

Chances are, you are reading this book because you love the dark, twisted side of history. There is also a chance that your fascination with the dark, twisted side of history has caused some of your friends and relatives to look at you in a funny way. They may even sit far away from you at the table on Thanksgiving, out of fear that you may feel compelled to talk about the death toll of the Johnstown Flood (2,209 lives lost, but you already knew that), or the type of automobile that Ted Bundy owned (Volkswagen Beetle, but you probably knew that too).

While your fascination with all things morbid may have led to alienation from co-workers or painfully awkward first date conversations, the good news is that you are not alone. Since its inception in 2012, my Pennsylvania Oddities blog has attracted (as of this writing) just under 2.5 million visitors, which means there are a lot of people just like you and me (or maybe there's only one devoted reader who visits Pennsylvania Oddities thousands of times each day).

As a general rule, blog writing needs to be concise to hold the attention of the typical online reader (not you), and, as a result, the strange and macabre stories I post on Pennsylvania Oddities provide just enough details to sketch a clear picture. Yet some of the more exciting stories, I feel, deserve to be told more fully, and this is how the book version of Pennsylvania Oddities came about. The following pages are filled with true tales of unsolved murders, mind-bending mysteries, harrowing hauntings, and other fun things you'll enjoy discussing at your next Thanksgiving dinner.

Of course, if you do decide to discuss some of the weird stories in *Pennsylvania Oddities, Vol. 2*, (and I hope you do) you should also be prepared to explain your fascination with dark history to those cousins, aunts, and uncles who have no idea how many lives were lost in the Triangle Shirtwaist Factory Fire (146) or the name of Elizabeth Báthory's husband (Ferenc Nádasdy, of course).

So, what is the point of studying the morbid and macabre?

It is my opinion that those of us who enjoy reading about such gruesome things are not "sick" or "twisted" at all. On the contrary, I believe that we are generally bright-eyed optimists who can appreciate just how far we've come as a society because we can look back and marvel at how cruel and callous the world was generations ago when it seemed like death was lurking behind every corner.

Most of us living today have been raised to respect life, and to show respect toward others, regardless of their gender, religious beliefs, sexual preference, physical and mental handicaps, socio-economic background, or ethnicity. As such, we find it difficult to comprehend why some people can do such terrible things other human beings, often without the slightest twinge of remorse. Imagine being a young woman in her early 20s, lacking formal education and working a menial job as a housekeeper, who finds herself pregnant after being seduced by a married neighbor, only to be deserted. Today, giving birth to an illegitimate child is not the end of the world, but to a young woman like Susanna Cox, who went to her death in Berks County in 1809, it was a burden too heavy to bear. Fearing the shame of becoming a social outcast and besmirching the good name of her family and employer, Susanna panicked and took the life of her newborn infant. It was a horrible thing to do, of course, but so was stringing up Susanna by the neck and leaving her to hang from the gallows for seventeen minutes before life was finally extinguished from her frail, quivering body. Such a needless double tragedy would have been prevented if only Susanna Cox had been born during the modern era.

And then there's the case of Frances Thomsen, a young schoolteacher and minister's daughter who murdered and nearly decapitated a sweet, elderly spinster in Luzerne County in 1931 because she became convinced (through messages she received telepathically) that the 76-year-old woman was operating a secret sex cult and trying to seduce her husband. Frances withered and died a few years later at the age of 41 in a mental asylum because society was unable, or unwilling, to recognize the signs of severe mental illness. Today, with the proper psychiatric treatment, someone like Frances Thomsen would be able to live a long, full life.

Of course, we still have a long way to go as a society before injustice, racism, disease, corruption, poverty and other ills and evils are vanquished, and if you browse the internet, scroll through social media posts or watch cable news long enough, you just might convince yourself that the world has gone to hell in a handbasket. But history—especially history of the strange, dark, and morbid variety—shows us that this is not the case. We no longer burn people at the stake for holding different religious beliefs. We no longer stone adulterers to death. We no longer remove chunks of a person's cerebral cortex to treat schizophrenia.

Sure, our work as a society is far from complete, but history tells us that we are on the right track. Slowly, but surely, we are making progress. We are a kinder, gentler, more tolerant society. And if you are one of those pessimists who choose to believe otherwise, then I strongly encourage you to read more historical stories about ax murderers, deadly diseases, and executions. It just might make you a happier, more optimistic person.

At the very least, it will give you something interesting to talk about during Thanksgiving dinner.

1.

THE HANGING OF SUSANNA COX

(BERKS COUNTY)

erks County was created in 1752 from parts of Philadelphia, Lancaster, and Chester counties, making it one of the oldest in the Commonwealth. Yet,—despite its abundance of rolling farmland—it is the ninth most populous in the state. Surprisingly, the number of executions that have taken place in Berks County since its creation is low compared to other populous Pennsylvania counties.

Among those who have died on the gallows are three women, the first of which was Elizabeth Graul, who went to her death on March 10, 1759. The second was Catherine Krebs, who was hanged on December 19, 1767. The last woman to be hanged in Berks County was Susanna Cox, who was executed on June 10, 1809. The crimes for which these young women paid the ultimate price were the same; all three women were found guilty of murdering their illegitimate infant offspring. Very little is known about the history of the first two women, but a considerable amount has been written about Susanna Cox.

Much of what we know today about Susanna comes from the records of Rev. Philip Reinhold Pauli, who, as pastor of the First Reformed Church in Reading, ministered to Susanna during her final days on earth and accompanied her to Gallows Hill, where she paid the ultimate price for her crime. Other details surrounding the execution were provided to local newspapers by those who witnessed the hanging. Some of these witness accounts, though printed decades after the event, are remarkably detailed, proving just how momentous that sweltering morning in 1809 was to the thousands who attended the sad spectacle—a spectacle that would remain etched in their memories for the remainder of their lives.

Susanna was the young, poor, and illiterate house servant of the family of Jacob Gehr, who lived in a large stone farmhouse in Oley Township. For eleven years, she served the family faithfully, but her country simplicity made her easy prey for men with less noble intentions. At the age of 24, after having been seduced and subsequently deserted by a lover, a married neighbor by the name of Martz, she found herself pregnant. In the cluttered mind of Susanna Cox, there were only two possible outcomes—live out the rest of her days as a social pariah, or infanticide. Confounding matters was the fact that Gehr and his wife, the former Esther Snyder, were from two of the oldest and most respected families in the county. Fearful of bringing shame to the household, she chose infanticide.

While the conditions of the crime may have aroused some sympathy for the young woman, any support Susanna may have had vanished when details of the gruesome crime emerged. An examination of the infant's body, which was discovered by Jacob Gehr, wedged into a crevice between the stones of the house, revealed that its jaw had been broken, the tongue ripped out, and a handful of straw shoved down its throat.

Nonetheless, Miss Cox pleaded not guilty when she was arraigned before Judge John Spayd on April 7, 1809. Four hours later (the judicial process being much speedier in those days), Susanna was found guilty. The following day she was sentenced.

While the crime committed by the young domestic servant was quite repugnant, so was the prospect of sending a female to the gallows. A petition was presented by Susanna's father, George Cox, to the governor, Simon

Snyder, asking him to spare her from execution. Governor Snyder, who was known for his compassion, gave serious deliberation to the matter. As fate would have it, the governor's opinion was changed on account of another young woman, Mary Meloy, who had also been facing charges of infanticide in Lancaster County (which was the state capital at the time). Although the way Meloy disposed of her child was even more gruesome, the jury decided to acquit, sparking outrage from the citizens of Lancaster County. Perhaps it was to appease the masses that Governor Snyder, on May 9, signed the death warrant calling for the execution of Susanna Cox, which was to be carried out on June 10.

As was the custom at the time, the execution of criminals was open to the public, and every county seat had its own "Gallows Hill." In Reading, it was at the head of Washington Street (on the site of present-day City Park), near the base of Mt. Penn. It was a spectacle that would be observed by a crowd of twenty thousand.

The day before the execution, Rev. Pauli administered Holy Communion to the condemned, in the presence of Sheriff George Marx. She was then presented with a white dress, trimmed in black ribbons, which had been sewn by family and friends. It was in this dress she would walk forth from her cell to the place of her death, and in which she would later be buried.

At eleven o'clock, the mournful procession, led by a troop of infantry under the command of Captain Lutz, moved forth from the jail and proceeded along Penn Street to Gallows Hill. The soldiers were followed by the prison officials, the wagon containing the coffin, and, lastly, the condemned and her aged spiritual advisor. It was a sweltering hot morning, and somewhere along the ten-block route, Susanna, leaning on the arm of Rev. Pauli, had to stop at a water pump for one last drink to slake her thirst.

At the gallows, Rev. Pauli offered a solemn prayer, after which was sung an old 17th-century German hymn:

I, wretched creature, sinner poor,
Stand here before Thy sight.
Oh God, show mercy in this hour,
Judge not with vengeful might.

Take pity, Lord, Thy Pitying God,
Upon my desperate plight.

Susanna then stepped up onto her coffin, atop the wagon which had been placed under the gallows, which were described as being little more than two tall wooden posts and a crossbeam. The masked executioner (whose name has been lost to history), covered Susanna's head and adjusted the noose around her neck. A second later, the signal was given, the horse hitched to the wagon was whipped, and the young murderess was swung into eternity, tightly clutching a white handkerchief in her hand.

Her neck was not immediately broken, however. The hangman, observing Susanna's clutched fist, acted quickly; leaping forward, he wrapped his arms around the girl's ankles and gave a yank to hasten her death. This drew an alarmed gasp from the crowd, who swarmed the executioner and threatened to lynch him from the very same gallows. An angry mob chased the hangman through the streets of Reading, finally catching him at the corner of Sixth and Penn, where he was beaten to within an inch of his life and robbed of the silver he had been paid to carry out the execution.

Whether the hangman's actions were rooted in sympathy or malice is still a matter of debate (I'm inclined to believe that he merely wanted to end the young woman's suffering. It's safe to assume that for many of the 20,000 assembled, it was the first time they had witnessed a hanging and probably weren't aware that the objective was death by a broken neck and not death by strangulation, which takes considerably longer).

Susanna Cox swung from the gallows for seventeen minutes before her body was cut down. After a physician pronounced her dead, the remains were turned over to relatives and buried at Thirteenth and Marion Streets, just west of Hampden Park.

2.

THE STRANGE HISTORY OF
MT. PENN'S FIRE TOWER

(BERKS COUNTY)

With its fieldstone construction reminiscent of a Medieval fortress, the William Penn Memorial Fire Tower is a Reading landmark that turns about as many heads as its Mt. Penn neighbor, the Pagoda.

While both structures are unofficial historical symbols of Berks County's largest city, the fire tower has a particularly strange history—a history marked by irony, tragedy, and perhaps even an Indian curse.

While the tower that sits atop Mt. Penn is seemingly ancient in appearance, it was built in 1938. It opened the following year to replace an earlier wood and stone tower that was constructed in 1889 by the Mt. Penn Gravity Railroad Company. This fire tower, as any Berks County historian is quick to point out, famously (and rather ironically) burned to the ground during the "Great Fire of 1923."

This tremendous fire, which swept the mountain on the evening of April 24, 1923, burned over 5,000 acres and, according to newspaper reports, was visible for over thirty miles. At the time of the fire, the mountain was a popular resort destination owned and operated by the Mt. Penn Gravity Railroad Company. It boasted a large dancing pavilion, bowling alleys, and concession stands, all of which adjoined the original fire tower. While the flames spared the nearby abandoned Summit Hotel, the other structures were destroyed, with losses to the Mount Penn Gravity Railroad Company surpassing $25,000 (the equivalent of $367,000 in today's currency).

This was a fatal blow to the company, which was already in a precarious financial situation; several years earlier, the company had been found liable for damages arising from a tragic 1890 accident that occurred at a curve on Mt. Penn (known locally as "Cemetery Curve"), when one of its railcars jumped the tracks and rolled down the mountainside, killing several passengers. A series of lawsuits followed, and the company was still paying dozens of survivors and families of the dead and injured victims at the time of the 1923 fire.

Because of the tremendous financial loss, the Mt. Penn Gravity Railroad Company decided not to rebuild the tower. This was probably a wise decision, as it seemed that every business venture pertaining to Mt. Penn was doomed to failure—and many people blamed these failures and tragedies on an old Indian chief who purportedly put a curse on those who attempted to conquer the mountain.

THE LEGEND OF THE BLACK SPOT

October of 1923 marked the city of Reading's 175th anniversary, and when local historians rummaged through the city's old records in preparation for the event, they came across an interesting local legend. As the legend goes, when the last Indian was driven out of the vicinity by early settlers, he made his last stand near the summit of Mt. Penn, and dramatically uttered a curse on the heads of the settlers. The spot where the Indian uttered the curse was said to be marked by black stones, which stand out in stark contrast to the white and gray rock native to the mountain. From that day forward, nothing has ever grown on "The Black Spot," which still exists near the site of the fire tower, and no business enterprise atop Mt. Penn has ever prospered.

As for the Summit Hotel, which was built in 1891 by brothers Henry and William Schwartz, it passed through a series of owners, all of whom found the hotel to be a financial boondoggle. It was abandoned for many years until the city purchased it in 1933. From 1933 to 1938, the city leased out the property as a bingo hall, before inexplicably passing a city-wide "bingo ban," thereby euthanizing its white elephant in the process.

Aside from the hotel, dance hall, bowling alley, concession stands, and gravity railroad, other failed ventures on Mt. Penn include Kuechler's Roost (an inn established in 1878 by Louis Kuechler, who was known throughout the region as "The Hermit of Mount Penn") which was destroyed by fire in 1919, Carl Schaich's winery and, of course, the Pagoda, which was initially built as a luxury hotel in 1908, but never opened.

While the original fire tower atop Mt. Penn is but a ghost of the past, some pieces of it live on; after the Great Fire of 1923, stones from the tower were used to construct the Skyline Boulevard retaining wall and can still be seen to this day.

3.

THE CAWLEY MURDERS

(ALLEGHENY COUNTY)

Across the river from Pittsburgh, on the southern banks of the Monongahela, lies the suburb of Homestead. Here, on a quiet street, lived a quiet boy named Charlie Cawley, a teenage genius who seemed destined to one day join the ranks of Thomas Edison, Alexander Graham Bell, and Cyrus McCormick in the pantheon of great American inventors.

It was 1902, and Charlie, a boy of just seventeen, already had a patent pending in Washington, D.C., for a new type of air brake. But there had been some kinks that he wanted to work out, and as summer evaporated into fall, Charlie's incessant work had driven him to the brink of mental and physical exhaustion. Adding to his frustration was the fact that it was difficult to find peace inside the tiny Cawley home, which Charlie shared with his mother, Hannah, and several siblings. Hannah had a total of 14 children; ten of whom were listed as alive on the 1900 US Federal Census. At the age of 20, brother James was the oldest, while baby Joseph, at 15 months, was the youngest. The other Cawley children fell somewhere in the middle, filling the air with all the sounds of youth: squeals of toddlers,

POLICEMAN ESCORTING THE YOUNG MURDERER TO THE BOROUGH LOCKUP.

Charles Cawley

the petty bickering of teenagers, the wailing of a baby, and the exuberant rough-housing of six-year-olds. It was enough to make a shy, introvert like Charlie lose his mind. How could he ever focus on his mechanical drawings and perfect his inventions with so much activity taking place around him?

Nevertheless, it was a happy, healthy family, and Hannah Cawley was proud of all her children. She was especially proud of Charlie, whose brilliant mind she was counting on to be the family's salvation. Maybe one day, one of Charlie's inventions would revolutionize the world and catapult the Cawleys out of poverty and out of the cramped quarters they managed to share without tearing each other apart. Her husband had met his death by drowning in the Monongahela at Redman's Mill just one year earlier, and life for the Cawleys had been a bittersweet struggle ever since. But Hannah held on to hope.

On October 9, Charlie made a maddening discovery: his papers and drawings had been stolen! A few weeks earlier, an unidentified Italian—a goon hired by the Westinghouse Corporation—had approached the young inventor and ordered him to stop working on his patent, or else he would see to it that Charlie was killed. The boy thought nothing of the man's threat at the time, but he was inconsolable after he found his papers missing after so many weeks and months of meticulous, nerve-wracking work.

At around ten o'clock on the evening of October 9, the Cawley family inside their six-room house at 414 Second Avenue (presently the site of The Waterfront) was preparing for bed. Mrs. Hannah Cawley and her twelve-year-old daughter, Belle, curled up together in one bed, while Joseph, Agnes, and the six-year-old twins—Adelaide and Raymond—clambered into another. Charlie, James, and Harold—the three oldest children—occupied a room adjacent to their mother's room.

It was around 3 A.M. when Charlie arose and got dressed, careful not to awaken his brothers. He did not put on his shoes. He tip-toed down to the cellar, grabbed an ax, and tip-toed back upstairs and entered his mother's room. There was a small kerosene lamp turned down low on the table next to Mrs. Cawley's bed, washing Hannah and Belle with a warm, yellow glow. Charlie stared at his mother and sister for a moment, watching their chests rise and fall in rhythm with their deep, peaceful breaths.

Mrs. Cawley's skull was crushed with the first blow of the ax. She never knew what happened, and in some strange, grim way, it was for the best. It was a mercy killing; Hannah would be spared the horror of witnessing the maniacal rampage that was to follow.

The thing about murder is that the hardest part is getting started. The hard part is taking that first stab of the knife, the first pull of the trigger, or, in Charlie's case, the first swing of the ax. But any murderer will tell you that the second blow comes easier than the first, and the third comes easier than the second.

Nobody was sure how many blows from the dull edge of the ax were delivered to Mrs. Cawley, but it was said that Charlie had beaten his mother's head to a jelly.

Isabelle, or Belle, as she was known to the rest of the family, had slept right through the murder of her mother. Charlie swung his weapon at Belle but missed, causing her to wake up. But before her young eyes could register what had happened, it was too late. The next blow killed her. But the blows kept coming... ten, fifteen, twenty, thirty... until the bedsheets and mattress were soaked in blood.

Beside the bed stood a crib where 15-month-old Joseph slumbered soundly. Charlie raised the ax high over his head. There was no hesitation, no swing and a miss. No need to deliver more than a single blow. Miraculously, the baby was still alive when Charlie left the room.

Next, he went over to the bed where Agnes, Adelaide, and Raymond were sleeping. Maybe Charlie's chopping had tired him out because the bodies of these children were still recognizable when the coroner came. For whatever reason, he did not bash them to a pulp as he had done with his mother and Belle.

Charlie entered the room where Henry and James, oblivious to the carnage in the adjacent bedroom, were sleeping. The creaking of the door caused James to awaken. The young man sat up, and in the faint yellow light of the gas lamp, he saw Charlie standing in front of him with an ax clutched tightly in his hand. The weapon was dripping with blood, and Charlie was splattered from head to toe with the gore of his victims. There was a maniacal gleam in the young inventor's eyes.

James knew he had to act quickly if he wanted to save his own life. As soon as Charlie closed the door, James extinguished the lamp, throwing the room into sudden, total darkness. He jumped out of bed just as the ax came crashing down. Charlie, who had not seen his older brother leave the bed, rained blow after blow on the mattress until he reached the point of exhaustion. James heard his brother mumble something he did not understand.

Charlie opened the door, and the room was once again illuminated by the glow of their mother's lamp. Seizing his opportunity, James lunged for the weapon as Charlie swung wildly at him. The ax grazed his arm and embedded itself in the bed frame. This only seemed to enrage the killer more; he dislodged the ax and rushed at James. James grabbed a chair as a shield. He sidestepped the next blow and then used every ounce of his strength to bash Charlie with the chair. A fierce wrestling match ensued.

James, who was three years older and much larger than his shy, timid brother, was taken aback by Charlie's strength. It was though demons possessed him. Eventually, James was able to pin down his brother and subdue him. As he dragged the murderer out of the room, he encountered the unspeakable horror that the veil of night had hidden, now revealed in the glow of the lamp. James later recalled that when he saw the blood-spattered walls and the dead bodies of his mother and siblings, he had to vanquish the urge to kill Charlie.

James dragged his brother through the streets of Homestead to the police station and turned him over to Officer Rosser. Charlie was placed in a cell. Rosser then returned with James to the Cawley house. Four of the victims were still alive at this time, and Harry—the only one of Mrs. Cawley's children home at the time who had avoided the slaughter—had already summoned Dr. Barton to the scene. The doctor made a grim pronouncement; they would be dead before sunrise. Another sibling, Mary, was spared from the attack because she was staying at the house of a friend.

It was reported that Dr. Barton removed two cups worth of crushed bone from the skulls of the victims. They were taken by train to the South Side Hospital to die.

Meanwhile, police chief West Noble had placed two officers on guard duty to keep away the curiosity seekers, but they had their hands full. Crowds flocked to the crime scene on Second Avenue, and relic-hunters desperately attempted to carry away a souvenir of the bloody crime. The crowds grew even larger the following day, with hundreds of visitors taking out pocketknives and trying to cut away slivers of the porch and siding. Others made off with chunks of the fence.

On Saturday morning, October 11, funeral services were held for Hannah and Belle Cawley at St. Mary Magdalene Church. They were interred at the church cemetery. Later that afternoon, the bodies of Annie and Raymond would be buried alongside them. Agnes and Adelaide were still clinging to life at the hospital, as was the baby, Joseph. Of these children,

Agnes would be the only one ever to regain consciousness. On November 4, Agnes had recovered sufficiently enough to leave the hospital, though she possessed no recollection of what had happened.

Warden Edward Lewis was perplexed. For days he had been observing the teenage ax murderer, looking for the slightest signs of guilt or remorse. But the boy in the cell remained calm. Not only that, but he also seemed to become more at ease with each passing day. When asked about the crime, Charlie told the warden that he had no recollection of it.

Detective P.J. Murphy also talked to Charlie but could discover no signs of insanity. He appeared content, healthy, and rational. He was eating well and sleeping without the slightest disturbance. The boy surmised that a burglar must have entered the house and slaughtered the family while they were sleeping.

Things took a strange turn on Thursday, October 16, after a man from Ohio came forward and identified the hero of the tragedy, James Cawley, as one of three men who had beaten and robbed him on the night of October 4. When the magistrate asked James if he was guilty of the charge, the young man nodded. Unlike his younger brother, however, James wept heavily when he was placed in jail.

This new development sparked a thunderstorm of rumors around Homestead. Did James play a role in assisting his brother in the savage slaughter of their mother and siblings? James had admitted to stealing a small sum of money from the man from Ohio after beating him, and Charlie clung to his belief that the killings had been carried out by a burglar. Was it possible that James Cawley, who had wrestled the bloody ax out of his brother's hands before dragging him to the police station, had set up Charlie to take the fall?

While thousands of men and women from the Pittsburgh area contemplated this issue, Adelaide Cawley passed away quietly, making her the fifth victim of the Homestead ax murderer.

Even experts were divided when it came to sorting through the mess. Two doctors—one of medicine and one of theology—interviewed Charlie and James in jail. Neither could agree on the identity of the real killer. The physician insisted that it was Charlie, while the theologist declared that it had to have been James. But all arguments ceased a week later when Charlie finally admitted to committing the murders.

There is a curious footnote attached to this part of the story; on the same day Charlie confessed; a letter arrived at the Cawley house. It was from the U.S. Patent Office in Washington. His air brake had been accepted, and all Charlie had to do to earn his patent was to pay a fee of $20. This, of course, was now an impossibility (he was eventually awarded a patent for his invention in November of 1902).

The killer's defense team was less than confident in a plea of insanity. By all accounts, Charlie was a model inmate while locked up at the county jail, awaiting trial. He showed no signs of remorse; nor did he show any signs of mental illness. According to the warden, he kept himself busy reading books. His attorney would later argue that Charles Cawley was a somnambulist—he had murdered his family while sleepwalking and, therefore, should be spared the death penalty. Charlie, however, had contracted tuberculosis during his confinement, and his relatives convinced the court to release the young killer into their custody so that he could die at home.

The strategy worked. Charles Cawley was acquitted of all charges. After his release, he was sent to live with his grandfather, Michael Cawley, an aunt, Mary McCue, and a sister, Mamie.

But fate caught up with the boy who had butchered his family. On Monday, February 20, 1905, Charles Cawley passed away from consumption at his grandfather's home on River Road between Beck's Run and Six Mile Ferry. Though his relatives did their best to keep the funeral arrangements a secret for fear of creating a public circus, it was later revealed that Charlie was cremated, and his ashes buried at the family plot at St. Mary Magdalene Cemetery.

Michael Cawley, the grandfather who had played an instrumental role in bringing Charlie home to die, passed away five days later.

4.

A TRAGIC GAME OF CARDS AND A CIVIL WAR MYSTERY

(FRANKLIN COUNTY)

The borough of Chambersburg plays an important, though forgotten, role in the history of the Civil War in Pennsylvania. While Gettysburg receives the lion's share of visitors and tourists, there is enough history in Franklin County's county seat to fill volumes. Chambersburg also played a role in numerous important chapters of American history, from the French and Indian War to the Whiskey Rebellion to the Underground Railroad.

Chambersburg also holds the distinction of being the only city north of the Mason-Dixon Line that was burned down by Confederate forces. The rebels had invaded the town on two previous occasions, but it was the order given by Gen. John McCausland on July 30, 1864, that reduced much of the community to ashes and smoldering rubble.

History records only one casualty resulting from the series of raids on the borough—a black resident who was trapped inside a burning building because the rebels refused to let him out. A few hundred Union soldiers were captured as prisoners, and two Confederate soldiers were reported as missing—and therein lies the heart of Chambersburg's most captivating unsolved Civil War mystery.

Early in the spring of 1902, workmen began construction on a new addition to the county courthouse. Part of the work involved excavating a well that was located behind the Hope Fire Company building. As the men began to dig, they were approached by an elderly resident who had a strange warning for the workers. The old man said that if the men were to dig down far enough, they would come across some human bones.

Sure enough, once the workers reached the bottom of the ancient well, they found part of a skeleton, along with a few brass buttons and a pair of buckskin gloves. Frank Henninger, who was overseeing the excavation, was curious to know how the old man knew that they would stumble across human remains.

The old-timer told Henninger a remarkable story. Not long before General McCausland gave the order to burn the town to the ground, one of his officers and a local resident were playing cards in the firehouse. The old-timer, who was just a young man at the time, was instructed to go out and purchase some beer for the gamblers. When he returned, he found that the Confederate officer had disappeared. The only player left was the Chambersburg resident, who explained that an altercation had broken out after he accused the Confederate officer of cheating. In a fit of rage, the Chambersburg man threw the rebel down the stairs. His neck was broken, and death was instantaneous.

Since it was just the two men who were left in the firehouse, the card player confessed to the beer-bringer that he had thrown the body of the dead officer down the well to conceal the crime.

The man who killed the officer moved away from Chambersburg years before the bones of his victim were found, his name forever lost to history.

As for the bones and brass buttons of the dead soldier, the May 2, 1902, edition of the *Harrisburg Telegraph* reports that Frank Henninger took them home as souvenirs.

But that's just one half of the story; records indicate that another Confederate officer was never seen again after the raids on Chambersburg. That officer was Major Bailey of Petersburg, Virginia. While his identity is known, the location of his final resting place remains a mystery.

Major Bailey was one of McCausland's finest men, but on July 30, while the town was burning, the young officer was shot. Because of the sheer madness and mayhem of the scene, the frenzied mothers dashing out of their blazing homes with babes in their arms, the frightened horses rearing and bucking, it was never clear who took the shot at Bailey or why. But, according to one eyewitness who was alive at the time—a local historian by the name of Noah Heckerman—the Confederate officer was picked up from Fairground Avenue, where he lay bleeding by a gang of angry locals.

The furious mob carried the officer down Main Street to Queen Street, and by the time the mob reached the public square, a large crowd had formed, and the crowd was hungry for revenge. Major Bailey, however, was not the kind of fellow to die without putting up a valiant fight. After a desperate struggle, he managed to break free from his captors, and, with every ounce of strength he could muster, he ran for his life, eventually arriving in front of the J.A. Eyster & Bro. general store (on the site that would later be occupied by Isaac Stine). Although the structure was a raging inferno, Major Bailey spied an opening through the fiery timbers and ran through, coming out on South Second Street. He eluded the mob by ducking into a white frame house next to the stable of Paul John's hotel.

Inside the house, the officer concealed himself in a pantry but had barely managed to close the door when the lynch mob caught up with him. Shots were fired into the door, and the crowd waited with bated breath. After a few moments, they opened the splintered pantry door and found that the Confederate soldier had been shot through the heart. According to Heckerman, the officer was still breathing as the mob dragged his blood-soaked body out of the house and onto the pavement, where he soon died.

Someone carried Major Bailey's corpse away in a wheelbarrow and hauled it to Harrison Avenue, where hundreds of Chambersburg residents viewed it. After everyone who wanted to had caught a glimpse of the slain rebel, the body was carted off to a lot owned by Jacob Shafer on South Second Street, near the offices of the Cumberland Valley Railroad, where it was buried.

It was a shallow, sloppy burial. Heckerman relates that the gravediggers were forced to scramble after it was reported that a detachment of Confederate troops was nearby. It proved to be a false alarm. Nonetheless, Bailey was sufficiently buried and remained in the Shafer lot until the end of the war.

After the war was over, Major Bailey's widow came to Chambersburg to claim the body, which she wanted to have interred in Petersburg. Unfortunately, she discovered that she didn't have enough money to cover the expenses. The citizens of Chambersburg, still angry about the torching of their city, sent her back to Virginia empty-handed and told her not to come back until she had enough money.

Meanwhile, the corpse of Major Bailey was dug up and re-buried behind the firehouse, on the grounds of the county courthouse. There was no gravestone to mark the spot, and no one from that time is still alive to point out the exact location of the unmarked grave.

Nearly two thousand Confederate soldiers marched into Chambersburg between the first raid on October 10, 1862, and the burning of the city on July 30, 1864. All of them returned to Dixie and lived to fight another day, except for two. And, strangely, the bodies of those two rebel officers came to rest just a few feet apart from each other behind the Franklin County courthouse.

5.

THE SECRET INDIAN TOMB OF PLEASANT HALL

(FRANKLIN COUNTY)

A centuries-old secret lurked beneath the Salem Lutheran Church in the Franklin County village of Pleasant Hall until it was finally discovered by workmen reconstructing the church in the spring of 1929. Even today, very few people are aware of the secret Indian grave located in the bowels of the church building.

The humble brick church that is visible today, a well-known landmark of Letterkenny Township, was built on the site of the original house of worship, which is believed to have been built in or around 1740. Although historians still debate the date of the original church's construction, it is evident that the church could not have been constructed before 1736, when Indians still held the title to that section of land.

Several decades later, a new church was erected on the same spot and continued to serve the Lutheran worshipers of the Letterkenny valley without interruption until major renovations took place in 1929, at the direction of Rev. W.J. Schultz. Among the scheduled improvements was the installation of a furnace, which required an excavation beneath the building.

It was during this excavation that the mystery tomb was discovered—the final resting place of, likely, a powerful Indian chieftain.

Unlike other burials of the region's indigenous peoples, the unknown chieftain was laid to rest in a tomb hewn to a depth of four feet in solid white stone. According to the workmen who unearthed the forgotten grave, only a few inches of the perpendicular end of the tomb were disturbed during the excavation. The construction laborers worked around the baffling and mysterious tomb, taking great pains not to cause any further disturbance to the sacred site. After they were done installing the new heating system, the workmen sealed the tomb behind a wall.

The identity of the once-powerful Indian chief remains unknown. He might have been a Lenape or a Shawnee warrior. Perhaps he did battle with the famed Indian fighter Major James McCalmont, the Upper Strasburg native who served during the Revolutionary War. According to legend, McCalmont was so skilled that, while running on foot, he could reload and fire his musket without breaking stride.

Years later, when McCalmont became a judge, he became extremely modest about his exploits as a frontier scout and Indian fighter, which, perhaps, only caused his legend to grow. He never admitted to killing an Indian, although he never denied shooting at them, either. However, it was understood throughout Franklin County that whenever Major McCalmont shot at a target, he seldom missed his mark.

Could the unknown chieftain buried in a stone crypt, hidden behind a wall beneath the Salem Lutheran Church, be one of Major McCalmont's victims?

Until the answer is discovered, this question will remain one of Franklin County's most remarkable unsolved mysteries.

6.

PREACHER GILL

(SNYDER COUNTY)

During the days of Prohibition, more than a dozen members of one notorious Snyder County family managed to keep lawmen busy around
the clock. This was the infamous Gill clan of West Beaver Township,
whose bootlegging exploits made headlines in newspapers across the state.

On November 22, 1924, a liquor raid occurred in Snyder County's
West Beaver Township, spearheaded by Mifflin County detective H.A.
Davis. The raid led to the arrest of John F. Gill—known throughout the
county as "Preacher"—and his three sons, who were charged by Detective
Davis with liquor law violations under the Volstead Act.

Though Davis was out of his jurisdiction, the raid near McClure was
"officially" conducted by the State Police, with Davis acting as director,
and a trial was held in Middleburg in December. It was an interesting
trial, to say the least; the Gills were acquitted after a gallon of "evidence"
was stolen from the courtroom sometime during the proceedings—even
though Judge Potter had ordered that the jug of moonshine and other

pieces of evidence be guarded at all times. Rumor had it that one or more of the jurors (or perhaps the bailiff whose job it had been to safeguard the evidence) had stolen the liquor out of resentment—a silent protest over a Mifflin County lawman's unpopular decision to stick his nose into Snyder County affairs. Or maybe one of the jurors was merely in dire need of liquid refreshment.

The *Altoona Tribune* even went so far as to indirectly accuse Judge Potter himself of stealing the evidence, while flat-out declaring that the Gill family was being shielded and protected by the corrupt law enforcement and court system of Snyder County. In fact, the *Tribune* ran its April 21 story on the Gill trial under the headline: *Snyder County Lawbreaker Evidently Enjoys Protection of Authorities.*

Public opinion toward the Gill clan was divided in the McClure area, however. During the arraignment hearing a month earlier, witnesses painted an unsavory picture of the moonshining family. One witness testified that Preacher Gill had once lined up half a dozen of his customers against a wall and pointed the muzzle of a shotgun at them while Mary "Ma" Gill looked them over. Her discerning gaze fell upon one customer. "That's the dirty rascal that stole five gallons of whiskey from us," she declared. Before the accused had a chance to protest, Ma Gill grabbed a broomstick and beat the man to the ground. The beating was so severe that the customer required five stitches from a local doctor.

Others rallied behind the Gill family. Neighbors praised Preacher Gill for his work preaching to a half dozen congregations of various denominations throughout Snyder County. But whether the citizenry loved or hated the Gills, everyone seemed to agree that Detective Davis had no business poking around outside his jurisdiction.

The Gills got their revenge on Detective Davis the following summer, however, after Ma Gill had Davis arrested, claiming that the Mifflin County lawman had damaged several valuable beehives and other property belonging to the Gill family during the raid. On August 3, 1925, Davis was arrested while attending the Belleville Fireman's Carnival by Constable Weirick and Deputy Runkle of Snyder County. This was most certainly payback, considering that Belleville is in Mifflin County.

Unfortunately for the Gills, their victory over the law was short-lived. Preacher Gill and two of his sons, Charles and Rush, were arrested for moonshining a short while later after another State Police raid. Rush fled the scene, leaving his father and older brother to stand trial before Judge Miles Potter, who was determined to make an example out of the notorious bootleggers after the press had smeared his name for showing too much leniency toward the family.

In late December, jail terms totaling 39 months and fines totaling $3500 were doled out to John "Preacher" Gill and his son Charles. The head of the family was sentenced to 21 months in the county jail while Charles earned a sentence of 18 months that same year. "You should've been convicted a year ago," the judge growled as he pronounced sentence, referring to the 1924 acquittal.

In January of the following year, Rush would be captured and subsequently sentenced by Judge Potter to 18 months in the Snyder County Jail. He would die a few months later, on March 19, 1928, just one day after his 34th birthday.

FEDS NAB LESTER GILL

In February of 1929, federal agents once again set their sights on the Selinsgrove area. On a cold, brisk Monday morning, they made their move, acting on tips provided by local informants. A lone agent, pretending to be frostbitten and "nearly frozen to death," asked around town where he could buy some alcohol. He was directed to the rural home of Lester Gill, one of Preacher Gill's younger sons. Near Schoch's Mill, the agent discovered a ten-gallon still and one hundred gallons of mash.

Surprisingly, despite the overwhelming evidence, charges against Lester Gill were dropped after a grand jury in Harrisburg decided to throw out the case, claiming that the prosecution of Lester Gill would create unfair hardship for his wife and seven children.

In January of 1930, as Preacher Gill, his wife, and their son Charles were cooling their heels in county jail, federal agents were putting together their case against the moonshining clan. Preacher Gill, now 67 years of age, would be sentenced by Judge Albert Johnson in Lewisburg to 18 months

Lester Gill and his wife

in a federal penitentiary in Atlanta, Georgia. He would later be transferred to Leavenworth. His son Charles would receive a 15-month sentence and would later be transferred to the federal prison camp at Fort Bragg, North Carolina.

As for Mary "Ma" Gill, she earned a slap on the wrist for her role in the family business and was sentenced to two years of probation, after managing to convince the court that she was suffering from tuberculosis and was in dire financial straits. The matriarch of the Gill clan, and mother of seven, died two years later at the age of 63. She was buried alongside her son, Rush, at Saint Peter's Cemetery in Troxelville.

PREACHER GILL DISCUSSES HIS PHILOSOPHY

It was during the 1930 trip to Atlanta that John F. Gill told his captors about how he came by his nickname. He revealed to Sheriff Crabb and the U.S. deputy marshal his unique philosophy—that moonshining and bootlegging are approved by Scripture. He spoke of Moses instructing his people to till the soil and reap the harvest, to pay their taxes and debts, and do whatever they please with the rest. Gill told his captors that he was following Christ, who had told the disciples to follow the law of Moses and, from Gill's point of view, Moses was basically telling the Hebrews that it was okay to make liquor.

"It is well that Christ lived 1900 years ago and not in this age," he added.

Preacher Gill, who had graduated from the old New Berlin Academy— a noted school of theology—refused to tell the lawmen whether he ever became ordained.

It was around this time that locals decided to launch a campaign to bring John and Charles Gill back to Snyder County. Just as "unknown person or persons" had stolen the gallon of moonshine from the courtroom in order to lead to the acquittal of the Gills, another group of unknown persons arrived in Middleburg in early March of 1930 to demand the parole of Preacher Gill and his son.

The McClure *Plain Dealer*, perhaps the only Snyder County rag that was staunchly unsympathetic to the Gill clan, wrote:

Just who the two upshoots are may not be made known as their identity for the time being is a secret, but what they are after is not the liberty of the Gills but their own interests. They want either to make money from their traffic or want their blighted appetite slaked by the free flowing of still more booze... The people of Snyder County, especially the western part, do insist that the law violators be prosecuted, and when sentence is announced, the prisoner serve his term.

A few years ago . . . the elder Gill was paroled with a plea of poor health to which even some doctors gave favorable evidence. Hardly was Gill out of jail until he was back to the old game, moonshining and bootlegging, and kept right at it even while under arrest and awaiting trial. Personally, the editor of this newspaper favors the serving of the term and rather than the parole of the Gills, arrest the balance of the bunch who are in the business.

In October of 1930, Charles disappeared from a federal prison camp at Fort Bragg after serving nine months of a fifteen-month sentence. Charles, who had been paroled, was ordered to report to Probation Officer H.J. Mowles in Selinsgrove. When a local reporter "informed" Mowles that Charles had taken a construction job in Virginia to earn enough money to complete his journey home, the probation officer laughed—the reporter, who concocted the story to cover for Gill, was unaware that discharged federal inmates are given free transportation home, a fresh suit of clothes, and $5 in cash.

Charles did eventually make it back to Pennsylvania, only to be arrested for moonshining again in 1935. He was sentenced to one year in jail and fined $200.

THE BALLAD OF FOSTER BOONIE

On a Monday morning in mid-June 1931, Vina Kauffman, a 29-year-old daughter of Preacher Gill, was doing the family wash in the kitchen of her home, about a half-mile west of McClure. As she stooped over to empty a basin of water, a gunshot shattered the kitchen window. "I'm shot!" she cried out, clutching her abdomen. Her husband, John, standing nearby, caught her as she fell. The bullet, believed by authorities to have been carelessly fired by a hunter atop a nearby hill a half-mile away, entered Mrs. Kauffman's back and penetrated the abdomen, piercing the liver and pancreas. She was taken to the Lewistown Hospital, where she remained in critical condition.

State Police were called from Lewistown. After examining the home, they went to the hospital where they obtained a statement from the injured woman, which led to the eventual arrest of a farmer and woodsman named Foster Boonie, who was charged with felonious assault and battery with intent to kill.

Boonie was arrested and taken into custody on June 23, after police discovered in his possession a gun of the type from which the bullet was fired. The detective in charge of the investigation found that the rifle had been recently fired, though Boonie protested his innocence. On the afternoon of July 7, 1931, Vina died from her injuries, and Boonie was re-arrested on a charge of manslaughter.

State Police troopers from Sunbury, who reluctantly made the arrest, believed that the 45-year-old farmer had shot Vina Gill Kauffman accidentally, arguing that it would have been impossible to hit a human target from such a great distance through a window. Snyder County authorities, on the other hand, perhaps in their continued support of the Gill clan, demanded that Boonie be arrested and charged with manslaughter, and claimed they had evidence of "difficulties" between the Boonie and Gill families.

The investigation of the shooting by State Police from the Lewistown barracks turned up additional evidence that seemed to exonerate Boonie, however. It was learned that Boonie had loaned the rifle to a friend on the day of the shooting for hunting crows. Boonie claimed to have been in Selinsgrove shopping at the time of the shooting, and witnesses who were interviewed corroborated Boonie's alibi. The investigators from Lewistown also learned that not only were the Gills and Boonies not quarreling, but that they were on good terms. The case against Boonie was eventually dropped for lack of evidence.

But that wasn't Boonie's last brush with the law. In April of 1932, Boonie was arrested after shooting his brother during an altercation at point-blank range and was sentenced to three years at the Western Penitentiary. Ten years later, Boonie strangled his estranged wife to death in Beaver Springs and mutilated her body. He died in the Snyder County woods in a hail of gunfire from a sheriff's posse in 1942.

Did Foster Boonie kill Preacher Gill's daughter, intentionally or otherwise? The truth may never be known.

It may be of interest to some readers that Foster Boonie and the wife he murdered with his bare hands (Grace Cordelia Hayes) are buried next to each other at Saint Peter's Cemetery in Troxelville, only a few yards away from the graves of Rush and Mary "Ma" Gill.

Vina's death must have had a profound impact on Preacher Gill, who had lost his wife and one of his sons just a few years earlier. From that day forward, the enigmatic leader of the notorious Gill clan began to distance himself from the family business—but his children and grandchildren carried on the clan's lawless legacy.

In November of 1933, Preacher Gill narrowly escaped death when his automobile overturned near McClure. The infamous bootlegger was trapped beneath the vehicle, but, fortunately, passing motorists were able to render assistance. Gill, who had been awarded parole nearly a decade earlier by convincing the court that he was a feeble old man in poor health, managed to escape without a scratch.

Preacher Gill's name appears to have vanished from the public record after that point, and it is unclear why he was never buried alongside his wife in Troxelville.

In 1935, the family Gill would be once again thrust into the spotlight—after the sensational murder of a farmer from Kantz by the name of Charles Gable.

THE WEDDING DRESS MURDER: DEVILED BY A TEENAGE LOVER

On February 18, a 29-year-old man named Sherman Strawser confessed to state police that he had killed his employer, Charles Gable, by bludgeoning him with a hammer and then shooting him in a barn as Gable was feeding his cows. Gable had fired Strawser just a few days earlier. Like the Gills, the Strawser clan was also a family of ne'er-do-wells from the mountains of Snyder County who were heavily involved in the moonshine business. Sherman's father was locked up in the county jail for bootlegging at the time of the murder, serving out his sentence alongside Charles and Lester Gill.

Strawser, who had twice been married and had children, had gotten Lester Gill's teenage daughter, Zella, pregnant, and the killer claimed that he been driven to murder his former employer to purchase a wedding dress for his 15-year-old lover. The Gill

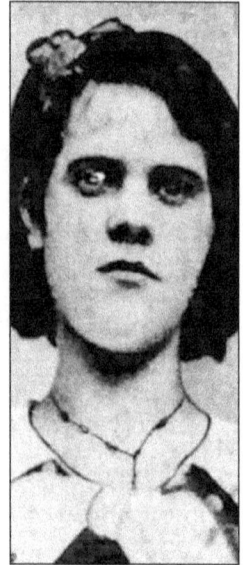

Zella Gill

family had made it abundantly clear what would happen to Strawser if he refused to marry Zella. In addition, the Gills wanted the money to bail Lester out of jail.

"Gill told me that if I didn't rob Gable and get money to get him out of jail, he would have me sent away for a long ride because Zella was with child and was under sixteen years old," Strawser confessed in court. He added that the Gill family had "deviled" him for days to commit the crime, with Zella and Mrs. Gill calling him a "baby" and a "coward."

Sherman Strawser was convicted of first-degree murder and died in the Rockview Penitentiary electric chair on July 22, 1935.

But the Gills were also facing charges in the death of Charles Gable. Police had discovered a wad of the dead man's cash hid-

Sherman Strawser

den beneath the stairs of the Gill house. Lester, along with his wife and daughter, would be forced to stand trial and fight for their lives.

LAWYERS NEARLY COME TO BLOWS IN SNYDER COUNTY'S TRIAL OF THE CENTURY

On June 7, 1935, a large crowd packed the Snyder County courthouse in Middleburg to witness the Gill trial. If an admission fee would have been charged, just about everyone who observed the proceedings would have agreed that they had gotten their money's worth. The testimony was fiery and contentious; the reporter from the *Mount Carmel Item* described Zella as "angrily snapping" her answers to John L. Pipa, the special prosecutor appointed by the state. She "defiantly spat answers at him," another local paper reported.

At times it seemed that the attorneys might even start throwing punches at each other. Pipa shouted at the defense attorney, J. Francis Gilbert, several times during witness examination. At one point, Gilbert even demanded that Judge Lesher ban Pipa from the courtroom.

Pipa, along with Attorney General Charles J. Margiotti, argued that Snyder County had a long history of showing favoritism toward the Gill clan, and accused Middleburg authorities of prejudice against Strawser. Sherman Strawser and Zella Gill, both present at the trial, refused to look at each other.

The Snyder County jury retired and soon came back with its decision. Once again, the Gill family was acquitted on all charges.

On the morning of July 22, Sherman Strawser walked to the electric chair and seated himself without assistance. He was pronounced dead at 12:35 A.M. Shortly before his execution, Strawser wrote a letter to his spiritual advisor. "Women can be a curse and again they can be a blessing," the condemned man wrote. "The last one has been a curse."

The 1935 execution of Sherman Strawser, paired with the repeal of prohibition in 1933, brought the story of the Gill clan to a close. As bootleggers across the nation turned their eyes to other pursuits, it appears that the notorious Gills of Snyder County finally did the same.

7.

THE CENTRALIA MYSTERY SKELETON

(COLUMBIA COUNTY)

When the calendar reads April 1 and a child reports finding a human skeleton in the woods, it's easy to dismiss the child's astonishing claim as a joke or a prank. That's precisely what happened to Oscar Fetterman, a 13-year-old boy from the now-abandoned mining village of Centralia, on April Fool's Day of 1917.

Oscar's story, however, turned out to be accurate, thus bringing to light one of Centralia's darkest unsolved mysteries.

Oscar was roaming the craggy, mine-scarred mountains near Centralia looking for teaberries on the day of his momentous discovery. When he reached the woods that divide Park Street and the Saints Peter and Paul Cemetery, his eye was attracted to something lying on the ground. He crept closer. It was a human skeleton, clad in dark clothing. A black derby hat and black dress shoes were next to the bones—a confusing choice of clothing for someone wandering through the woods.

Leaving his berries behind, the boy ran back to Centralia as fast as his legs could carry him and told anyone who would listen about his gruesome find. Everyone thought it was an April Fool's prank, of course. Still, Oscar's story spread throughout the small town, eventually attracting the attention of two men, Walter Kimmel and an unidentified friend, who said that since they were going past the cemetery later that day anyway, they would take a look for themselves.

Kimmel and his friend easily located the skeleton, and the cemetery's undertaker and the county coroner were summoned to the scene. They concluded that the man had been dead for about six months. They examined the dead man's clothing but were unable to find anything that could be used to identify the remains.

As word of the discovery spread throughout the area, a Shamokin man by the name of Joseph Stack traveled to Centralia to view the remains. His son, James, had mysteriously disappeared from home six months earlier. Upon seeing the remains, however, Stack concluded that it could not possibly be his son; James was tall, and the bones were too short. He also examined the scraps of clothing found in the woods and did not recognize them.

Joseph did provide authorities with a possible lead, however. He told investigators of a fellow from Johnson City (which is presently known as Ranshaw) who also disappeared around the same time. Relatives of the missing man came to view the remains, but once again, the remains didn't fit the description. Since there were no other reports of missing persons from the area, the bones were gathered into a box and buried in an un-marked grave in the Aristes cemetery, a few miles away (It's unclear why the bones weren't buried in the Centralia cemetery where they were discovered. I guess that since the Centralia cemetery belonged to the Greek Orthodox church and all the parishioners were accounted for, the church didn't want anything to do with them).

Although more than a century has passed, the mystery skeleton of Centralia remains unidentified—and since the bones were buried in an unmarked grave, it appears that the mystery will forever remain unsolved.

Today, thanks to an underground mine fire that has been burning since the early 1960s and will probably continue to burn for generations to come, all that remains of the once-thriving ghost town are a few deserted streets, crumbling foundations, and the Saints Peter and Paul Cemetery, where a poor, unfortunate fellow met his mysterious demise in 1917.

8.

DEATH OF A CANDY MAN

(SCHUYLKILL COUNTY)

Unpunished murders have always been a blight on Schuylkill County's colorful history, especially during the 1920s and 30s, when gangsters and organized crime terrorized the Coal Region of Pennsylvania. The official record indicates that between 1925 and 1932, the lives of eight Schuylkill County individuals were snuffed out by killers who have never been caught. In some cases, the murderer was identified but eluded capture, disappearing into the night, never to be seen again.

The peculiar death of William Laughlin remains another unsolved Schuylkill County mystery—more than three-quarters of a century after it took place.

Nobody had seen William Laughlin since Tuesday, March 25, 1930. After three days had passed, a group of fifty local men, led by several police officers, scoured the woods and mountains around Barnesville looking for the 39-year-old man. This beloved fellow worked as a confectioner at his father's candy shop in Centralia. Laughlin's body was discovered a day later, on Saturday evening, in a most unusual place—inside a concession stand near the entrance of the now-defunct amusement resort known as Lakewood Park, which was located in Barnesville about a mile away from the Lakeside Ballroom.

Mysteriously, Laughlin's lifeless body was found in the nude. An autopsy held in Tamaqua revealed that the man had died of a broken neck caused by a sudden blow to the back of his head. But one thing struck police as being even more mysterious—police had searched that very concession stand only one day earlier, thereby indicating that his dead body was carried there sometime between Friday evening and Saturday.

William Laughlin, accompanied by eight friends, had traveled to Lakewood Park on Tuesday night to watch a boxing match between Pat Igoe and Mickey Diamond. After the match, he and his friends parted ways. He did not return with John McGinley, who had driven him to the park.

However, a night watchman named William Ault reported that an unidentified man was seen later that evening, wandering the park grounds barefooted and in short sleeves. This was odd, considering that March evenings in the mountains tended to be quite chilly. The watchman attempted to stop the wanderer, but he disappeared into the darkness of the night, making a positive identification impossible.

But on the following day, a coat and hat were found on park grounds, and these items were identified as belonging to William Laughlin. A watch was found inside the coat pocket, along with a book of matches and a pack of cigarettes. Both the hat and jacket were dry and clean, even though it had rained hard during the night. Not even the matches or cigarettes were damp.

Immediately, officials ordered the dam opened, and the lake drained, suspecting that the missing man might have drowned in the park's 10,000,000-gallon reservoir. On Friday, the day before his body was located, Laughlin's socks and shoes were discovered. Strangely, the socks were dry, but the shoes were soaked. Stranger still was the fact that both items had been located along the lake shoreline, on the grounds that had been thoroughly searched earlier.

After the autopsy was complete, the body was taken to the home of his father, John P. Laughlin, who owned a popular candy shop in Centralia.

The funeral was held Wednesday morning, April 2, at St. Ignatius Church, and he was laid to rest in the parish cemetery. Laughlin's wife, Clara, had died three years earlier. He left behind one seven-year-old daughter, Mary Louise, along with three brothers and two sisters.

According to local papers, the concession stand where Laughlin's body was found was a two-room bungalow, situated near the edge of the park along the state highway. During the tourist season, the bungalow served as a concession stand as well as a fortune-telling booth. The front of the bungalow featured a porch, enclosed with screen netting, and it was on this porch where the body was discovered, with a pair of pajamas pulled down around Laughlin's ankles.

The case was handled by Mary Jones of Tamaqua, the first female deputy coroner of Schuylkill County. It was Jones who ordered the post-mortem examination, which showed that Laughlin's death—most likely caused a blunt object—could not have been accidental.

The subsequent investigation by the Tamaqua detail of the Pennsylvania State Police also revealed that robbery could not have been the motive; his gold pocket watch had not been removed from his coat pocket. Despite a massive search, Laughlin's trousers, vest, and underwear were never found.

Not everyone believed that Laughlin's bizarre death was murder. Some speculated that Laughlin might have been struck by an automobile after he left the boxing match while walking from the pavilion to John McGinley's car. McGinley waited around for his passenger and, when he didn't appear, decided that he must have gone off with other friends. According to this theory, Laughlin, severely injured, wandered the park grounds in a dazed condition until he arrived at the bungalow near the entrance. Those who believed the hit-and-run theory speculated that Laughlin was still alive after police had first searched the bungalow on Friday, and continued to ramble the grounds, clinging to life and shedding his clothes, while the search for his body was taking place.

But this theory fails to explain why Laughlin's shoes were found wet and his socks were found dry, or why the victim's body was found in the nude, with his pajamas pulled down to his feet. And why hadn't a search party of fifty men and police officers been able to locate the rest of his clothing? Might it be possible that these missing items could have yielded an important clue about the killer?

On April 16, a coroner's inquest was held at the town hall in Tamaqua. At the hearing, no new evidence was presented, but the jury dismissed the hit-and-run theory, rendering a verdict declaring that William Laughlin "came to his death as a result of violence administered at the hands of a person, or persons, unknown."

In early May, authorities hinted that arrests were "imminent" in connection with the mysterious murder, stating that "substantial clues" had been uncovered, possibly placing Laughlin at a nearby hotel on the night of his disappearance. This development proved to be a false lead.

Then, in early June, State Police once again intimated that arrests in the case were forthcoming. According to the June 7, 1930, edition of the *Shamokin News-Dispatch*: "The police have been working quietly on the assumption that Laughlin was killed in a hotel near the park. Arrests are to be made within the next few days, it is said."

And, once again, police failed to make good on their promise. This was the last time the mysterious death of William Laughlin was written about, and the case seems to have quickly faded into obscurity.

As for Lakewood Park, it, too, faded into obscurity. It was never as popular or as well-managed as Lakeside Park, with its famous ballroom that is still in operation, which was located less than a mile away in Barnesville. While Lakeside Park had been around since 1880, Lakewood didn't come into existence until 1916. The 88-acre park, owned by Richard and Daniel Guinan, also boasted rides, concessions, and a swimming lake just like its rival down the road.

To steal the wind out of their older and more successful neighbor's sail, the Guinan brothers opened the Lakewood Crystal Ballroom in 1925—exactly one year to the day Harry Hart opened the Lakeside Ballroom. And, in a display of one-upmanship, the Guinans made sure their dance floor was slightly bigger than that of their rival (Lakeside's dance floor measured 144 by 80 feet while Lakewood's floor was 168 by 104). Lakewood Park closed in 1984, and the Crystal Ballroom burned down in 1998.

When Lakewood Park closed, its grand carousel was sold to an amusement park in Michigan, where it continues to operate to this very day. And when the weather warms, and the soft breeze of summer whispers seductions of buttered popcorn and candy apples, perhaps some child in Michigan will take a ride on a carousel pony whose glass cabochon eyes may have once witnessed the mysterious murder of a candy man from Centralia.

9.

AN ARMLESS FRUIT VENDOR AND
A POTTSVILLE MYSTERY

(SCHUYLKILL COUNTY)

A t the north end of North George Street in Pottsville, just a few hundred yards from Nativity BVM High School in the part of town
known informally as Lawton's Hill, once stood the home of John
Weaklem, invariably described in late 19th century records as the "armless
fruit dealer of Norwegian Street." In Weaklem's backyard once stood a pear
tree, where the body of an unknown infant was hastily buried in 1894, and
records suggest that the remains of this unfortunate infant are still there
today, in an unmarked grave.

As to the identity of this child, and the cause of death, these facts
remain an unsolved Schuylkill County mystery.

What little facts we do know are these: John Weaklem first learned
of the matter from Deputy Coroner James J. Clemens, who had been informed of the burial by Weaklem's son, Al, and his wife.

Weaklem had shared his home with his elderly mother and a daughter named Clara, who filled the role of Weaklem's housekeeper until October of 1893 when she moved to Philadelphia. Since the handicapped fruit seller was unable to take care of domestic matters on his own, his son and daughter-in-law moved into the Weaklem house at 341 George Street.

One day, Al's wife (who was also named Clara, incidentally) was looking for a shirt and began rummaging through the bedroom that was formerly occupied by Clara Weaklem. She noticed an offensive odor coming from the dresser, and she brought the matter to the attention of her husband. Upon further investigation, Al and his wife found that the foul smell was coming from a bundle of cloth in one of the dresser drawers. They untied one end of the bundle and gasped in horror when the light of day revealed its shocking and unexpected contents—the bones of an infant. All the flesh had been eaten away by worms, which were also still inside of the bundle. Horrified and sickened by their discovery, they immediately took the bundle outside and buried it in the garden beneath Mr. Weaklem's pear tree.

They never told Weaklem what they had done, because the incident surely would have put the spotlight of guilt upon Clara. However, Al and his wife felt obligated to report the matter to the authorities.

When Deputy Coroner Clemens visited the house on George Street and questioned Mr. Weaklem about the dead infant, he was overwhelmed with grief and shame. Although he claimed to know nothing of the matter, the news was a devastating blow. Could this have explained why his daughter Clara, now estranged to him and the rest of the family, had packed up in the middle of the night and ran away to Philadelphia three months earlier?

The strange turn of events saddened even Deputy Coroner Clemens. As a merchant, Weaklem was one of Pottsville's most beloved and respected citizens. Despite his handicap, he worked tirelessly to support his aged mother and to raise his children to become responsible, upstanding members of society. And now the Weaklem name risked being tarnished by this gruesome, baffling tragedy.

Although a thorough investigation was made, from the state of the remains it was impossible to tell whether or not the child had been dead or alive when it was born, or when it was tied up into a bundle and hidden in the dresser drawer.

As for Weaklem, he stated that he didn't even suspect that Clara was pregnant or romantically involved with anyone. He knew nothing of her whereabouts, other than that she had gone to Philadelphia, and she had not made any effort to contact him. The authorities attempted to track her down but came up empty-handed. Apparently, she was now living under an assumed name, a name that she would carry with her until the end of her days, which were no doubt haunted by memories of what she had done, and the persistent fear that, one day, the law would catch up with her.

Unfortunately for the unnamed babe in the dresser drawer, it never did.

Faced with a dilemma, Deputy Coroner Clemens ordered the remains to be left undisturbed, and, to the best of anyone's knowledge, that is where they remain to this day—on a hilltop in Pottsville inside an unmarked grave.

10.

EATABITE TIBBS

(FAYETTE COUNTY)

From Babyface Nelson to Prettyboy Floyd to the Sundance Kid, crime and colorful nicknames go hand in hand. While these outlaws may be more famous or their exploits more sensational, few criminals have been endowed with a nickname as unusual as Angus "Eatabite" Tibbs, the eccentric and charismatic bandit who terrorized western Pennsylvania in the late 19th and early 20th centuries, while managing to escape from mental asylums and jailhouses and surviving gunshot wounds that would have killed a normal man along the way.

Eatabite Tibbs first earned notoriety as a result of Uniontown's Jasper Augustine scandal of 1895. Augustine, a wealthy and influential member of the local community, was arrested for keeping "a disorderly house" and was sentenced in November to one hour of jail and a $500 fine. The investigation revealed that Augustine's brothel was frequented by many of Pittsburgh's most prominent politicians and businessmen. These revelations, along with the striking beauty of the madam, Jessie Davis, created a media sensation. The courtroom circus continued for months, culminating in Augustine's wife filing for divorce and Augustine's attorneys alleging that a business rival had framed Jasper.

Many civic leaders, prostitutes, and petty thugs were caught up in the Augustine scandal, and among them was Eatabite Tibbs, who just a young ruffian at the time. The June 14, 1895 edition of the *Pittsburgh Daily Post* reported:

> Another phase of the case was the trial of Samuel Magie, a wealthy liveryman; Mell Baxter and "Eatabite" Tibbs, the latter two negroes. The men were charged with assault and battery upon R.P. Kennedy, Augustine's attorney. Magie was acquitted, but the colored men were convicted.

During the trial, Eatabite stood up and complained that one of Jasper Augustine's witnesses had been threatening him, but he was shouted down by Judge Mestrezat. Infuriated, Eatabite returned to the courthouse fifteen minutes later with a revolver and said that if the court wouldn't protect him, then he would have no choice but to protect himself. He was promptly sentenced to nine months in a workhouse for carrying a concealed weapon. There, he convinced his jailers that he was insane and attempted suicide by hanging himself. He was transferred Dixmont mental asylum, from which he escaped a few weeks later by pulling a gun on the guards. Tibbs later claimed that it was one of Jasper Augustine's associates who had helped him concoct and execute the insanity ruse and subsequent Dixmont escape by providing him with a rope and a gun. One account of his daring escape appeared in the *Connellsville Weekly Courier* on August 9, 1895:

> The police authorities of Pittsburgh and Fayette County were notified last Friday evening to endeavor to recapture Angus Tibbs, a negro, who escaped during the morning from the Dixmont Insane Asylum. Tibbs is known in this county as "Eat-a-bite," which name he is said to have acquired through his cannibalistic habit of chewing people in his numerous fights. He came to Uniontown from Roanoke, Va.,

during the coke workers strike over a year ago. He worked for a short time, and then began to assume control over the negroes. After he was sent to the Work House, "Eat-a-Bite" shammed insanity and made his actions so annoying that a petition was presented in the Fayette courts for his removal to Dixmont.

CANNIBAL OR PIE-EATER?

There is some debate as to how Angus Tibbs earned his unique sobriquet. While newspapers were fond of reporting that he was called Eatabite because he liked to use his teeth during fights, others have claimed that he had been called "Eat-a-Bite" from an early age because of his ferocious passion for pies and pastry. One account stated: "He ate pies by wholesale. A strange freak of fate had so shaped his face that he could swallow a pie without breaking the crust or spilling the juice."

On the evening of March 17, 1896, a shootout took place on the outskirts of Uniontown between Eatabite Tibbs and local lawmen, who finally caught up with the escaped asylum inmate after he burglarized a house and attempted to kill Judge Mestrezat earlier that evening.

It was Judge Mestrezat who had sentenced him to nine months at the Claremont workhouse for carrying a gun the previous summer, and revenge was never far from Eatabite's mind. On Tuesday night, Tibbs drank freely of liquor, and with each glass, his hatred of the law deepened. Finally, he got up and left the saloon, declaring to witnesses, "I'll fix him now." Concerned bystanders passed the word onto the police, who spotted him just outside of the judge's home. As luck would have it, the officers were already searching for the outlaw, who was believed to be behind a break-in in another part of Uniontown.

When Tibbs saw the officers, he ran away down Railroad Street and was headed for the Catholic church when Constable Murphy ordered him to halt. Eatabite jumped a fence, stumbled, but regained his footing just as the posse was closing in on him. He dashed across the church graveyard but, by this point, he had lost his steam. With the law hot on his heels, he stopped in his tracks, turned, and opened fire.

The officers fired back with a volley of gunshots that lasted ten full minutes. Twenty-two shots were fired. Tibbs finally staggered forward and fell to the ground with two bullet wounds in his body. One of the bullets entered his right shoulder, while the other entered his chest and lodged in his lungs. He cursed the officers as they attempted to arrest him, fighting them off with flying fists and furious feet and vowing that they'd never take him alive. At the jail, a doctor examined Eatabite and pronounced the wounds to be fatal and that the outlaw would be dead by morning. Eatabite laughed and said he'd recover. He was right.

Nevertheless, Tibbs was now facing more than 30 separate felony and misdemeanor charges for his asylum escape, burglary, attempted murder of a judge, and shootout with the police. If convicted, Eatabite Tibbs faced a prison sentence of 105 years.

On June 8, Eatabite was tried and convicted but was sentenced by Judge Ewing to just four years at Riverside Penitentiary (which later became known as the Western Penitentiary). A week later, as Tibbs was being delivered to the prison by Sheriff Chalfant, a crowd of hundreds showed up to catch a glimpse of the infamous outlaw, whose daring exploits had turned him into a local celebrity.

Four years later, just as his sentence was set to expire, Eatabite Tibbs was transferred back to Fayette County Prison to await sentencing for his armed robberies. Tibbs, however, had other plans.

THE SOUP CARRIAGE ESCAPE

On October 1, 1900, Tibbs became the first person to escape from the stony walls of "Old Fayette" successfully, and he pulled off this feat without having to resort to violence, dynamite or hacksaws. Tibbs simply stepped onto the elevator, rode to the basement, and casually walked out through an unlocked door. It was a plan that was ingenious because of its astonishing simplicity, and only a person with Eatabite's bravado and brazen personality could pull it off without a hitch.

Inside the jail, Sheriff George McCormick had installed an elevator connecting the kitchen in the basement with the first, second, and third tiers of cells. The elevator was used to deliver meals to the inmates, who referred to it as the "soup carriage." Although the doors to the elevator were securely locked, Eatabite had been granted a small measure of freedom because of his "trusty" status, which granted certain privileges to well-liked and well-behaved inmates.

According to reports, jail officials had grown to like the eccentric Eatabite, who was said to entertain the other prisoners with jokes, songs, and funny stories and was very helpful and cooperative with the prison staff. But just as he had feigned insanity to execute his first escape, the congeniality was just an act designed to win his captor's trust. Escape had been on Tibbs' mind since the day of his arrival.

Eventually, Eatabite's trusty status earned him the job of transporting meals to the inmates. Although he wasn't permitted in the basement or inside the "soup carriage," he was granted access to the corridor, which led to the elevator. On the day in question, he waited for the right moment and then jumped on top of the elevator carriage as it descended to the basement.

The guards, led by Deputy Sheriff A.Y. Stum, gave chase to the fleeing convict through the woods and up the ravine known as Coon Hollow, but couldn't catch up with Eatabite. Stum later recalled that he and the other guards could have shot Eatabite, but they were all too fond of him to kill him.

For reasons unknown, Sheriff McCormick suppressed word of Eatabite's escape from the press, as well as from the citizens of Fayette County who had no idea that a dangerous, erratic, and notorious outlaw was on the loose. Although the jailbreak occurred on October 1, 1900, the public was not made aware of the escape until October 24, when the *Pittsburgh Post-Gazette* reported:

> There are a number of persons who would feel decidedly uneasy if
> they knew Eat-a-Bite has the freedom of the town, and perhaps it
> was to prevent such apprehension that Sheriff George A. McCormick
> decided to not advise the public of Tibbs' exit from the stone fortress
> of 'Old Fayette.'

EATABITE DEFIES DEATH AGAIN, GRANTS BEDSIDE INTERVIEW

At around 11 P.M. on Sunday, October 4, 1903, a man named Charles Stratton was returning to Uniontown from Connellsville on a streetcar when he was shot in the arm by an attacker identified by Stratton as Eatabite Tibbs.

According to Stratton, he and Eatabite had both been courting the same girl from Connellsville, and Tibbs had threatened him on several previous occasions to stay away from her. Stratton said that Eatabite had been stalking him all weekend and had grabbed a seat just behind him on the streetcar when it stopped at Wheeler. At the Mt. Braddock stop, Tibbs approached the conductor, Evan Jeffries, and said, "Mr. Jeffries, I have a gun." Stratton claimed Eatabite said no more after that; he simply pointed the gun at Stratton, shot him in the right arm, and then jumped from the car.

When officers attempted to arrest him in Uniontown, Eatabite, as usual, tried to escape. He was shot through the back and then taken to Cottage State Hospital, an armed guard stationed outside his room. Because the lead ball was located right next to his heart, doctors decided that it would be too dangerous to attempt its removal. Eatabite proudly claimed that he could feel the ball every time his heart beat.

Reporters flocked to Cottage State Hospital to talk to Eatabite, who loved seeing his name in print nearly as much as the newspaper editors themselves did. In 1955, George H. Moore, the revered Pittsburgh newspaperman, reminisced that the two most significant days in his 60-year news career were William McKinley's election in 1898 and the shooting of Eatabite Tibbs. "Tibbs was always good copy, he was in trouble so much," Moore recalled.

Confined to a hospital bed recovering from yet another gunshot wound that would have claimed the life of a lesser man, Tibbs granted an interview to a reporter from the Connellsville Weekly Courier. When asked about his next possible escape, Tibbs said that escaping from Cottage State Hospital would be easy enough, but he planned on staying put for the time being. "A man must hide, and a man must eat," he stated. "Eating is one of the biggest considerations when you are trying to get away from the law."

He was then asked about his infamous soup carriage escape from Old Fayette.

"Mr. McCormick has been blamed for letting me go, but that wasn't any fault of his. It was simply because Eatabite was too smooth for the prison people. I had that thing framed up to make a general delivery that time, and if those boys in jail had any sense, they would have gotten out. If Bill Sims had been a brave man, he would never have hung, for I showed him how to get out when I left. Ed Spinner was in then, and both he and Sims were sentenced for murder. I told them the night before that I was going out the next morning and asked them to come along."

Eatabite said that he only ever divulged his plans and methods to murderers, adding that he didn't waste his time with the "short term men." As for the origins of his nickname, Tibbs said that he made it up himself while he was living in Cheat Haven to scare the local children. "I used to tell them that I would eat them up. 'My name's Eatabite!' I used to holler at them," he explained. "And the name stuck to me."

He told the reporter that even though he had been shot through the back, he could've gotten away if he wanted to. After shooting Tibbs, Officer Jesse Shaffer put his revolver on the ground as he knelt next to the outlaw. "I was still able for a good run, and I could have stopped Shaffer easily with his own gun. But I liked him. He's too good a fellow to shoot."

The nurses at Cottage State Hospital adored Eatabite, telling the press that he was one of the best patients they had ever taken care of. Tibbs was later sentenced to 12 years for shooting Charles Stratton and was once again hauled off to Western Penitentiary.

THE ECCENTRICITIES OF EATABITE

Tibbs is of a very peculiar character. He is possessed of an intelligence far above the average Negro and is well versed in the Scriptures. He claims to be a servant of Satan, and no one seems to doubt that he is. He is always ready to do anything for a friend, but the one who incurs his ill will had better prepare for trouble. —*Connellsville Daily Courier*, Aug. 5, 1904

Eatabite could hold a grudge better than anyone, and in 1905 he was delighted by the news that his old Fayette County adversary, Judge Ewing, had been killed by the No. 3 train as he attempted to cross over the tracks between Fayette Street and Jefferson Street in Uniontown. Eatabite collected every newspaper clipping of the judge's demise, and from inside his cell, he built a wooden model of the spot where Judge Ewing had been killed. Working entirely from memory, he constructed an exceptional model, depicting every detail of the vicinity, every building and sidewalk in the area, and even built a miniature model of the No. 3 locomotive. Tibbs wanted to paste a picture of Judge Ewing on the exact spot where he had been killed, but none of the newspaper clippings featured a photograph of the victim, so Eatabite drew the judge by hand. By all accounts, it was an accurate and good likeness of Judge Ewing.

For Tibbs, finding ways to kill time was the hardest part of being in prison. In addition to building models and drawing pictures, he also fancied himself as an inventor. In November of 1906, he unveiled a plan for a six-horse wagon that could be pulled by a single horse. Claiming that his invention would "revolutionize the world," he attempted to find an investor who could secure him a patent (there were no takers). He also passed the time by dabbling in mysticism and claimed to have discovered the secret to eternal life:

> Eatabite Tibbs, a Fayette County inmate of the Western Penitentiary, has written a Uniontown man that by taking a certain letter of the alphabet and adding it to one's name, he or she will be assured of eternal life. Eatabite says he can point out just what letter is necessary in each case. —*Pittsburgh Weekly Gazette*, Nov. 22, 1905

Unfortunately for Eatabite Tibbs, his study of the occult and Scripture couldn't ward off the dreaded disease of tuberculosis, which he contracted during his incarceration at Western Penitentiary. In early October of 1913, the 41-year-old inmate sent for Rev. P.H. Thompson of the Mt. Olivet Baptist Church in Uniontown. Eatabite had a strange but simple request of the pastor; he asked Rev. Thompson to preach his funeral sermon—while he was still alive to hear it. The reverend declined.

As Eatabite's health deteriorated, he was sent to the home of his sister, Mary Ferguson, in Steelton, Dauphin County, to spend the remainder of his days.

Sadly, no newspapers remarked upon his death, which records showed occurred at Steelton on December 14, 1913. He is buried in Culpeper County, Virginia.

For all the things that have been written about him, the fact remains that Eatabite Tibbs never killed anybody, though some may speculate that this had less to do with intent and more to do with lousy marksmanship. Eatabite himself probably believed that he never caused trouble for anybody unless he felt they deserved it, and, had fate been a little more kind, Tibbs might have gone down in history as a folk hero of sorts. He certainly had the personality and charisma for it. At any rate, Angus "Eatabite" Tibbs holds a place as one of the most fascinating and unusual outlaws in Pennsylvania history.

11.

THE HAUNTED CABIN OF JUMONVILLE

(FAYETTE COUNTY)

Just east of Uniontown, in Fayette County, is Jumonville, famous for its 60-foot-tall cross, which protrudes from the top of Dunbar's Knob. Built in 1950, the enormous cross is visible from fifty miles on a clear day and can be seen from three states. Jumonville is also home to a Methodist retreat center, which sits on the site of an old orphan's school that was created by the state of Pennsylvania to care for the children of Civil War soldiers killed in battle.

In the late 19th century, there was another point of interest that made Jumonville famous—a mountain shack haunted by the ghost of a boy who was strangled to death.

In early January of 1896, the surrounding towns and villages were buzzing with rumors of a peculiar haunted cabin in the woods near Jumonville, and a party of volunteers decided to pay a visit to the shack and see if the rumors and legends were true. Many volunteered, but as the appointed day of the investigation grew nearer, most of the folks had suddenly lost their bravery. Eventually, a party of a dozen strong-willed men was organized and, armed with old muskets, they ventured to the site of the alleged haunting.

The January 18, 1896, edition of the *Allentown Leader* described the event, which might very well be the first organized "paranormal investigation" in the history of Fayette County:

> They had not waited long within the dingy old walls when strange and unearthly sounds were heard in the old kitchen in the rear of the building. The stoutest heart quailed, but they crowded closely together, each feeling secure in each other's company. Gradually the moanings came nearer and grew louder.
>
> Things were about to get spookier. Much, much spookier. According to witness accounts, the sounds seemed to be that of a strangled child. The group then observed a phantom-like figure which appeared in the doorway, but instantly vanished. A few of the men in the party claimed they saw what they believed to be two ghostly figures engaged in a life-or-death struggle. One of the party said he could see armless hands clutching the throat of a child, and being unable to bear the sight any longer, he rushed screaming from the house.
>
> The other members of the party followed in his footsteps, beating a hasty retreat through the rugged forest and eventually coming to a halt near a stand of trees at the edge of a clearing. They weighed their options and eventually arrived at the conclusion that it was not worth going back to the cabin for another look. They had seen more than enough.

As for the haunted cabin, historical records indicate that it was built by Robert Fulton, a soldier who served under General Edward Braddock during the ill-fated Braddock's Campaign in the summer of 1755. After the war had ended, Fulton's stone cabin became a popular hangout spot for local youngsters, where they gathered and danced the night away.

It was during one of these dances that a gruesome murder took place. William Wise, a brutish woodsman, was highly intoxicated during the dance. A young boy who lived down the mountain near the Wise home-stead had been informed that William's wife had fallen gravely ill. The boy ran miles through the woods and up the mountain to relay the message to Wise, begging him to leave the party and return home. Wise didn't give much credence to the boy's plea; instead, he refilled his glass with cider. The boy refused to give up, however, and this apparently angered the backwoods brute. Wise grabbed the boy by the neck and slammed him to the floor. By the time he released his grip, all life had been extinguished from the innocent messenger.

William Wise, as it turns out, was never arrested for the crime, even though he had a reputation for being close friends with some of the most heartless thugs whoever called Fayette County home. One of Wise's closest companions was a man by the name of John McFall, and the two men spent countless hours in the mountains in pursuit of lost Indian treasure. Wise and McFall were often seen trudging through the wilderness armed with picks, shovels, and a treasure map.

McFall later murdered a tavern owner named John Chadwick during a dance at Fulton's cabin on November 16, 1794 (some historical records, such as the memoirs of early settler Robert A. Sherrard, claim that Mc-Fall murdered Chadwick inside the latter's tavern) by bludgeoning him to death with a wooden club. After his arrest, McFall escaped from the jail by burning a hole through the wooden door of his cell while the guards were sleeping. According to legend, McFall used his own urine to extinguish the fire before fleeing into the mountains. He was captured a few months later, tried, convicted, and hanged, thus earning the dubious distinction of being the first person executed in the county.

Not long after John McFall's execution, William Wise took his own life with his old, trusty musket. Perhaps he was filled with guilt and remorse for murdering the poor boy who had ran through the woods to relay the message of his wife's failing health. Or perhaps he believed that justice was about to catch up with him, just as it had caught up with his old treasure hunting buddy. At any rate, the lives and deaths of John McFall and William Wise have passed from local history into Fayette County legend.

12.

THE LOST CHILDREN OF THE ALLEGHENIES

(BEDFORD COUNTY)

In the spring of 1856 one of the saddest chapters in the history of Bedford County was written, after the two young sons of Samuel and Susanna Cox (not to be confused with the woman of the same name who was hanged in Reading in 1809) wandered away from home and into the mountains. The search for the two boys, aged five and seven, lasted for two weeks and culminated in a gruesome discovery beneath a large tree on the shady banks of Gypsy Creek. And had it not been for a prophetic dream, the whereabouts of George and Joseph Cox might remain a mystery.

The strange tale of the lost children of the Alleghenies began on the morning of April 24, 1856, when the boys followed their father into the woods. Samuel Cox, who had just finished breakfast inside the family's primitive log cabin in Spruce Hollow, grabbed his rifle after he heard his dog barking. The dog had managed to tree some small animal, and Samuel, desperate to put meat on the family table for dinner, bolted from the cabin.

He was so eager to shoot the trapped animal that he failed to notice that George and Joseph had followed him outside.

Life had been hard for the Cox family. Samuel and Susanna had been married in Johnstown and left shortly after the birth of their first child, George. Filled with the pioneer spirit and desperate to make their way in the world, they went to Indiana, which was largely wild and unsettled at the time. After a few hard years, they returned to Pennsylvania and settled in Bedford County. Samuel Cox cleared a plot of ground in the howling wilderness of Spruce Hollow, in the extreme northwestern section of the county, near the intersection of the Cambria, Somerset, and Blair county lines.

Wilderness stretched for hundreds of yards in every direction of the Cox cabin. At night, the cries of panthers and mountain lions pierced the mountain air; during the day, rattlesnakes sunned themselves on boulders and logs. It was a dangerous place, but Samuel viewed it as paradise. On the morning of April 24, guided by the barking of his dog, Samuel shot and killed the large squirrel that had been trapped up the tree. He decided to return to his cabin by taking a different path. It was a fateful decision he would live to regret; by taking a different route back to the cabin, he missed the two young boys who were attempting to follow in their father's footsteps.

By nightfall, a search party consisting of over a hundred men and boys began scouring the woods for the lost children. This is remarkable and demonstrates how neighbors looked out for one another back in those days. Even though the telephone had not yet been invented, and even though the nearest neighbors were a half-mile away, every able-bodied man in the region dropped whatever they were doing and rushed to offer their assistance to the panicked family. By the time the search was over, more than 2,000 residents of Bedford, Cambria, Somerset, and Blair counties had taken part.

Yet, despite the tenacity of the search party, very few clues were found. Many different theories were advanced. Some insisted that a band of gypsies had kidnapped the two boys. Others believed a gang of bandits had sold the children into slavery. Still, others pointed their fingers at the Cox family, accusing the parents of murdering their own children. The prevailing opinion, however, was that wild beasts had devoured the children.

As the search stretched into its second week, hope began to wane. But Samuel and Susanna refused to give up; they were willing to try anything that could lead them to George and Joseph. They employed the services of an old Negro who had a local reputation for being a voodoo witch doctor. The old man claimed that he could find the lost boys using a divining rod made from the forked branch of a peach tree. When this failed, they turned to a woman in Somerset County who dabbled in the "black arts" and supposedly had certain supernatural powers. After two unproductive days, the woman was sent back to Somerset County.

On the tenth night after the Cox children went missing, a young man who lived fifteen miles away had a strange dream. This man was Jacob Dibert, who would later fight in the Civil War. Dibert dreamed that the two little boys were lying under a birch tree next to a mountain stream. Dibert had not taken part in the search and had little familiarity with the terrain, so he quickly forgot about his vision. But on the eleventh night, he had the same dream. This time it was a little clearer and seemed more realistic. On the twelfth night, the dream came again, and in the morning, he told his wife about the disturbing vision.

Dibert's wife, who had been born and raised in the wilds of Bedford County, thought she recognized part of the landscape described by her husband. She relayed the details of Jacob's dream to her brother, Harrison Whysong. He told the search party about his brother-in-law's prophetic vision, but they laughed.

On the fifteenth day, Dibert and Whysong ventured into the wilderness alone. Whysong believed that the stream in Jacob's vision was located about seven miles from Spruce Hollow. In the dream, there was a fallen log spanning a swollen creek, and the men found a log like the one in the dream spanning Bobb's Creek, which was swollen from the melted mountain snow. The men crossed over and found a path. Dibert said that soon they would encounter the carcass of a deer laying across the path. Sure enough, a few hundred yards along the trail, they found the dead deer. They were getting close.

According to Jacob Dibert, the boys were asleep beneath the branches of a birch tree. In the dream, the tree was different than the others surrounding it. The trunk was bent and twisted, the top of the tree was split as if a bolt of lightning had once struck it. Dibert and Whysong continued along the path until they spotted the tree from the young man's dream.

And there, beneath the branches, they found the lifeless bodies of George and Joseph Cox, who are still remembered to this day as the "lost children of the Alleghenies." The children had apparently died of starvation.

Jacob Dibert was given a cash reward for finding the lost children that had been offered by a group of concerned citizens from Bedford County, which he turned over to the grieving parents. It was this reward money that Susanna and Samuel Cox used to purchase the tombstone that marks the graves of George and Joseph at the old Mt. Union Cemetery, and to erect a stone monument at the site where the lost boys of the Alleghenies were found through the prophetic dream of Jacob Dibert.

The monument marking the spot where the children were found was made and erected by C. Benson Culp of Schellsburg and can still be seen today at Blue Knob State Park. The monument is simple and elegant in design and consists of a square shaft with a pyramidal top. Inscribed on the memorial are the words:

> The Lost Children of the Alleghenies Were Found Here May 8, 1856, by Jacob Dibert and Harrison Whysong. Joseph S. Cox, Aged Five Years, Six Months and Nine Days; George C. Cox, Aged Seven Years, One Month and Ten Days. Children of Samuel and Susanna Cox. Wandered from Home April 24, 1856. Dedicated May 8, 1906.

As for the man who had the prophetic dream, he would die in Virginia at the age of 42 during the siege of Petersburg. Although a monument bearing his name can be found at Mount Zion Cemetery in Bedford County, his mortal remains are buried in a mass grave near the Point of Rocks battlefield.

13.

THE DISAPPEARANCE OF ALICE ARNOLD

(PERRY COUNTY)

When four-year-old Alice Arnold disappeared from her Perry County home in the spring of 1911, it sparked one of the largest search missions in the history of Pennsylvania. The search, which lasted for two months, involved hundreds of volunteers, dozens of police departments, an Indian tracker from the Carlisle Indian School, and even a clairvoyant. The formal investigation was officially closed after a child's skeleton was later found on top of a mountain, on a well-traveled path, but the evidence seems to suggest that the human remains which were laid to rest in an unmarked cemetery plot were not those of Alice Arnold at all. Combined with the cryptic, often contradictory statements made by the girl's family, the case of Alice Arnold just might be the most baffling unsolved mystery in Pennsylvania history.

It was Monday morning, May 22, 1911, when little Alice was last seen alive at the Arnold family home at Marsh Run, near Ickesburg. By nightfall, a search party of two hundred volunteers had scoured the dense underbrush and mountains but, as the search stretched into its second day, not a trace of the little girl could be found. They did, however, discover footprints in the vicinity belonging to a mountain lion or panther, and the consensus was that Alice had been dragged away by a predator of the four-legged variety.

Rain fell heavily on the second day of the search, but the volunteers, undeterred by mud and muck, pressed on, desperate to locate the little child who was beloved by everyone in Marsh Run. Neighbors began to fear for the health of Mrs. Arnold, who appeared to be on the brink of nervous prostration. The day ended with no clues or leads, and Alice's mother began to fear the worst.

Alice was the pride of the household, the youngest of the seven Arnold children. Bright-eyed and fair-haired, she was last seen wearing a brown gingham dress and no shoes, indicating that she hadn't planned on straying very far from home. She was last seen by two brothers, Clarence, age 7, and James, age 10, who were driving some cows through the woods on Monday morning when they heard a child's footsteps behind them (a conflicting report stated that it was Mary, age 6, and not Clarence who was with James).

At any rate, the older siblings told Alice to go home having no doubt about her safety; though Alice was young, she, like all the other Arnold children, knew the hills and valleys surrounding the family homestead well. By the time Clarence and James returned, Alice had already been reported as missing, and thirty-five neighbors were searching the nearby hills and woods. Concerns over Alice's safety were raised around 8:15 that morning when two woodsmen, Nevin Herr and Danny Lesh, heard a little girl weeping approximately 300 yards from the Arnold home.

On Tuesday, local authorities attempted to procure bloodhounds, but the nearest bloodhounds were miles away in Harrisburg, and the day's search ended before the dogs arrived. By Wednesday, May 24, volunteers from Newport, New Bloomfield, and other surrounding communities had joined in the search. The group of approximately 200 men formed a single line and advanced through the woods one step at a time, ringing bells and blowing bugles. Another group of thirty searchers focused on a stretch of forest near Donnelly's Mills, while a third group covered the wilderness around Run Gap. A neighbor named Ira Smith said that he would ring the big bell on top of his barn to inform the others should one of the parties locate Alice first.

The determination of the searchers was astounding. One of the volunteers, John F. Reisinger, was in bed recovering from burns he had received a few days earlier fighting a forest fire when he learned of the missing girl. On Tuesday, he pulled himself out of bed to help find Alice Arnold, combing the rugged mountains with his badly burned feet in bandages. The pain he must have felt with each step is unimaginable; it was reported that his bandages were thoroughly soaked in blood when he returned home later that evening. Nonetheless, he assisted in the search each day until its completion.

But not everyone in Perry County showed the same spirit, unfortunately. A nearby lumber camp, populated by foreigners, refused to join in the search. Naturally, many saw their reluctance as a sign that one or more of the lumbermen may have played a part in the girl's disappearance.

THE STATE POLICE JOIN THE SEARCH

In all this time and in all the number of miles covered, not a single trace of the missing baby has been found. The disappearance is as complete as though the earth had opened to swallow the baby and then had closed again. —Harrisburg Telegraph, *May 25, 1911*

On Wednesday evening, the parents implored Lt. Ed Wetzel of Harrisburg to get the State Police involved. Sergeants Curtis Davies and Francis Markey were soon on the scene, along with a tracker from the Carlisle Indian School by the name of Sylvester Young. They used the home of Danny Lesh as their headquarters, while the throng of newspapermen fought amongst themselves to procure a room at tiny Rice's Hotel in Ickesburg.

By the start of the following week, the State Police had become convinced that Alice was no longer alive in the Tuscarora Mountains—it seemed that every square inch for miles in every direction had been gone over with a fine-tooth comb. Foul play was now their leading theory. Davies and Markey told the press that they had a few possible suspects under

Search party members in front of the Arnold home

surveillance. They had interviewed dozens of locals and found conflicting stories regarding the missing child.

By Monday, May 29, volunteers were no longer looking for signs of life, but signs of death. Policemen explored the vicinity for signs of recently churned soil that might indicate a burial. Others kept watch from adjoining hilltops, scanning the skies for a circle of buzzards. Streams and rivers as far away as Duncannon were dragged for the missing girl's body. Sylvester Young, the Indian tracker, announced that he had found a leaf stained with blood not far from the Arnold home.

MR. ARNOLD TURNS TO A CLAIRVOYANT

With Mrs. Arnold hobbled by heartbreak and incapacitated by grief, it seemed the only one who believed that Alice was still alive was her father; over the weekend, he had traveled to Harrisburg to hire a fortune-teller, Madame Black.

The fortune-teller said that Alice had been kidnapped by gypsies, whose camp lay between two streams of water. Alice, according to the fortune-teller, had been carried off by a man with a large, black beard.

Madame Black, who probably had a little gypsy heritage herself, told Mr. Arnold that the child would be returned unharmed if he offered the gypsies a large cash payment. She also predicted grave injuries for Sylvester Young, the Indian tracker, if the ransom was not paid.

Another new development was the implication of James Arnold, the ten-year-old brother of the missing girl who had told her to go home on the day of her disappearance. The boy told the newspaper interviewers several different versions of what had happened. In one version of the story, Alice refused to go home, so James struck her on the shoulders with a stick. The State Police gave little credence to the theory that James had accidentally struck and killed his sister, however. It was unlikely that a boy of such a young age would have the physical strength or presence of mind to dispose of Alice's body in such a way that 200 expert hunters and woodsmen could not find it.

On Tuesday, May 30, the commissioners of Perry County offered a $100 reward for any information leading to the discovery of Alice Arnold. Law enforcement began to track down the movements of every gypsy camp, in the unlikely event that Madame Black was privy to some dark, supernatural secret. Police departments and railroad employees across Pennsylvania were told to be on the lookout for any suspicious party traveling with a yellow-haired girl with blue eyes.

CHARRED BONES AND A MYSTERIOUS BUGGY

Later that morning, a startling discovery was made. At around ten o'clock, Sylvester Young, accompanied by State Policemen Davies and Markey, found charred human remains on the top of a mountain only a mile and a half away from the Arnold home. The bones were hidden beneath a pile of logs. The policemen believed that the body had been recently burned. After Trooper Markey examined the bones, he hastily declared that they were those of a female child. However, he was immediately bitten by a snake that had been hiding among the logs and had to leave the investigation to seek medical attention.

Since there were no other reports of missing children in the vicinity, it was widely reported that the remains of Alice Arnold had been found.

The official announcement would have to wait until after Dr. Bryner had examined the bones in Harrisburg. Meanwhile, acting on an anonymous tip, the State Police searched the Arnold home as well as the home of the child's uncle, Albert Arnold.

On Wednesday, May 31, Dr. J.H. Bryner announced that the bones found on the mountain were not those of a human after all, but of a dog. Later that evening, about an hour before midnight, witnesses in the village saw a horse and buggy racing at breakneck speed on the path leading away from the Arnold home. Trooper Markey of the State Police and Sylvester Young ran out of the Lesh house and commanded the driver to halt, but the buggy was already out of sight. It was the belief of many that the speeding buggy was carrying away the dead body of Alice Arnold.

Two days later, the State Police called off the search, however, though they offered the people of Ickesburg their assurance that detectives would continue working on the case if new clues were discovered.

THE CRYPTIC STATEMENTS OF THE ARNOLD FAMILY

Even though the authorities had turned their attention to other matters, the story of Alice Arnold's disappearance was still closely followed by the press. The Arnold children were hounded incessantly by reporters from the *Harrisburg Telegraph* and other local papers. Alice's parents and siblings made more than a few eyebrow-raising statements to the reporters, which continued to keep the story on the front pages.

"My mother thinks she knows where Alice is, but she won't tell me," said Clarence Arnold to one reporter.

"Some people say that we know all about the child, but we don't know anything," Mrs. Arnold insisted to another.

"I don't believe in dreams, but last night was the first I have dreamed for months," said Mr. Arnold. "I dreamed that I was sitting on a chair in the room over there when suddenly I heard a window in the next room open softly, and the next moment, I heard Alice's voice saying, 'Mama, Mama, let me in.' I could hear the child knocking against that door. I made a grab for a revolver and was going after the person who brought the

Mr. and Mrs. William Arnold and James and Mary Arnold, the two children last with Alice Arnold, in front of their home near Ickesburg.

child and put her in the window when I was awakened. That dream has impressed me very much."

Even Samuel Arnold, a brother of Alice's father who was in western Pennsylvania when Alice went missing, couldn't get his story straight. When he came back to Ickesburg a week later, he was immediately asked if he had heard about Alice's disappearance. He appeared shocked and surprised and said that no one had yet told him of his niece's disappearance. Yet he told another person that he raced back to Perry County after receiving a letter from his mother telling him about the girl's disappearance.

Reporters tracked down Samuel's mother (Alice's grandmother), who was sharing a home with Albert and asked her about this conflicting account, but she grew livid and refused to speak to the press. Albert, the brother of Mr. Arnold, whose home had been searched by the State Police a week and a half earlier, claimed that he had watched his mother write the letter to Samuel, but she had never mailed it. When he volunteered to show it to the reporters, his mother became furious and threw the reporters out of the house. (I'm inclined to believe that Samuel had to have known about the disappearance of Alice Arnold. The story had already been picked up by newspapers across the country by the time he returned to Ickesburg in mid-June. As for the peculiar behavior of Alice's grandmother, no satisfactory explanation has ever been produced.)

THE POSTMISTRESS' TALE

On June 17, a possible clue emerged from the village of Etters in York County, fifty miles south of Ickesburg. The town's postmistress claimed that a few days earlier, she witnessed an Italian couple dragging a small child fitting Alice's description through town. The barefooted girl was wearing a ragged dress, and her hair had been cut short, but the postmistress was certain it was her.

Although it had not been made public until after the postmistress came forward with her story, the State Police had followed a lead three weeks earlier when a Millerstown resident told them that an Italian couple had been seen in the village with a little girl on the day of Alice's disappearance. Captain Lumb of the State Police immediately dispatched a trooper to Etters to investigate. Lumb stated that his trooper had managed to trace the trail of the Italians from Etters to York, where they boarded a train to Harrisburg. Witnesses told the policeman that the blonde-haired child was struggling to get away from the Italian couple all the way to the station.

But things took a surprising turn a few weeks later when a girl's skeleton was discovered on Tuscarora Mountain.

On the afternoon of July 19, Alvin and Harvey Wallett and Miles Zimmerman were picking huckleberries on the mountain, approximately three miles from the Arnold home at a spot known as Snake Hollow, when they found the remains. The men marked the spot and then raced back to Ickesburg to notify Justice of the Peace C.J. Swartz. Swartz sent the men back to guard the body until the authorities arrived and then empaneled a jury to hold an inquest. A different account was given by the *Harrisburg Telegraph*, which stated that Wallett rushed to the Arnold home immediately after finding the skeleton, and Mr. Arnold identified the remains by the hair and dress before Swartz was notified.

The Newport newspaper, on the other hand, reported that Swartz then picked up Mr. and Mrs. Arnold so that they could identify the body. Unfortunately, by the time all parties reached the mountain nightfall had set in, and the berry pickers who discovered the corpse were unable to find it again. They searched until 3 A.M. before giving up.

THINGS AREN'T ADDING UP

The following morning, they returned to the top of the mountain and found the body in a clump of brush growing in a large clearing devoid of trees. Many thought that it was strange to find the mortal remains of the little girl in that spot because it was at the junction of three well-traveled paths, and the area had been combed multiple times by hundreds of volunteers. Several members of the original search party told the *Telegraph* that they had searched the very same spot on previous occasions, and they scoffed at the notion that a 4-year-old child could have reached that spot on the boulder-strewn mountaintop on her own power.

Common sense supports this theory; the average walking speed of a 6-foot-tall adult on flat terrain is approximately 3.1 miles per hour. An average four-year-old child is about 40 inches tall, or half the size of a fully grown adult. Factoring in Alice's size and the uphill climb she would have to have made (hungry, scared, and barefoot, no less), it would have been virtually impossible for her to reach the clearing on top of the mountain, three miles from her home, in under three hours. By that time, more than fifty local searchers would have already been scouring the mountains.

Also strange is that several newspapers described the girl's clothing and hair that does not match any of the reports given previously. By all accounts, Alice Arnold had light blonde hair and had worn a brown gingham dress when she disappeared. Yet one newspaper account from Newport states:

When found yesterday afternoon, her body was scattered over about six feet of surface, all the flesh having disappeared excepting a small portion at her hips.

Her little pink dress and some of her hair, which was auburn in color, were found, leaving apparently no doubt as to her identity.

Nevertheless, the inquest hastily concluded that the body was indeed that of Alice Arnold and that the child's death had resulted from "want of food, thirst, and exposure." On Friday, July 21, she was buried at St. Paul's Cemetery in Eshcol. To mark the spot where the remains were found, a large pine tree near the site was painted white, and a streamer was affixed to the trunk as a monument.

Sadly, Alice May Arnold was buried without a grave marker. Because the cemetery records were destroyed in a fire, the location of her final resting place—if it really was Alice Arnold's bones found on the mountain— remains a mystery, along with the actual cause of her tragic death.

14.

A MURDER IN LIBERTY VALLEY

(PERRY COUNTY)

For most of his 63 years on earth, Hugh Smith was a respected resident of Liberty Valley. Hugh, along with his brother Sam, owned 380 acres of land in Perry County, and he earned a handsome living renting out his lands to sawmill operators. And for 28 of those years, the respectable Hugh Smith may have carried with him the belief that he had gotten away with the perfect murder.

It was Sunday, March 14, 1869, when Malinda Snyder wandered away from her home in Liberty Valley. Her disappearance had caused little alarm at the time; the 20-year-old, described as being a "half-witted mute" of about two hundred pounds, had a habit of wandering aimlessly throughout the valley. Days passed, and she never returned, and it was accepted as fact that the poor young woman had perished from hypothermia somewhere in the Tuscarora Mountains.

The years passed, and everybody had long forgotten the fate of Malinda Snyder. Everybody except for Elias Snyder, the missing girl's brother, that is. On March 8, 1897, Elias finally decided to break his silence. He claimed to know what had happened to his sister, and he told his story to the local magistrate, S.B. Trostle.

On the day that Malinda had disappeared, there had been a fire in the valley. One of the local sawmills had burned to the ground. According to Elias Snyder, his sister had gone to visit Hugh Smith that very day, and the sawmill that burned on the day of the girl's disappearance was one of the many that stood on his Perry County property. There had been an accomplice, said Elias, who claimed that Malinda had been hanging around the Smith house and refused to go home. This angered Hugh, who picked up a hatchet and, in a fit of rage, drove it into the friendless woman's brain.

Smith was alarmed at the horrible deed he had just committed, sickened and shocked by the brutality that he didn't even know existed within him. With the aid of an accomplice, Smith decided to conceal the crime. The two men put their brains together and came up with a plan. If they were to set fire to the Kendig & Co. mill, they knew that the attention of the entire neighborhood would be focused on the inferno, allowing them an opportunity to conceal the evidence of Hugh's horrible deed. As every soul in Liberty Valley flocked to the scene to witness the blaze, the killer and his accomplice used the cover of darkness to transport the lifeless, bloodied body of Malinda Snyder to an old, overgrown farmstead nearby that had been long abandoned.

In the middle of the field, there was a decrepit, dilapidated house, and this house had a large, old-fashioned stone chimney. While the accomplice kindled the fire, Smith hacked the dead girl to bits and pieces. Before the sun had come up the next morning, all that was left of Malinda Snyder was ash.

The magistrate told this story to District Attorney Kell, who convinced Sheriff Johnson and Constable Bistline to arrest Hugh Smith for the long-forgotten crime. He was arrested and taken to the Perry County jail, where he shared a cell with a horse thief. These two men had plenty of room to stretch out their legs, for they were the only two prisoners in the county jail at the time.

Smith's oldest son, Sylvester, who was around 38 at the time, was firmly convinced of his father's innocence, however. After a detrimental story about Hugh appeared in one of the local papers after the arrest, the son encouraged the accused murderer to tell his side of the story. From a legal standpoint, this was a major gamble, and any defense attorney worth his salt would have strongly advised against it; one poorly worded statement could be enough to send Hugh to the gallows. On the other hand, the right story could soften the hearts of potential jurors before the case even went to trial.

Hugh began his story by telling the newspaper reporter that he had been married twice and that his first wife had died some years earlier. He fathered thirteen children, ten were still living, and three were dead. If the prominent Liberty Valley resident was playing for sympathy, he was off to a good start. The March 8, 1897, edition of the *Harrisburg Daily Independent* wrote of the jailhouse interview with Smith:

It was a touching scene as the old man, six feet more in his stockings, with matted beard and hoary locks, stood before the interviewer and, with tears in his eyes, told his version of the tragedy.

Hugh Smith stated that he knew Malinda Snyder well and that the girl's father was a good friend of his. He also claimed that he was in bed and sleeping at the time of the sawmill fire and learned about it the following day. This statement, however, is difficult to believe, as the Kendig & Co. sawmill was only fifty rods from his house. This part of Smith's story was also later contradicted by several witnesses.

"This is all a piece of spite work," Hugh declared. "There are some neighbors of mine who think they can make something out of digging up an old charge that was gossiped about nearly thirty years ago, but there is nothing in it. I have nothing to hide."

When asked if Smith had ever ordered Malinda Snyder off his property, he replied: "I never spoke a cross word to her in my life. Why, see here—I helped nurse that little girl when she was a wee little thing. Her folks all knew me and liked me.

"Young man," concluded the accused killer to his interviewer, "be sure to tell the people I am innocent, and I will always swear that."

After speaking to the Harrisburg reporter, Smith "lawyered up" and retained the services of two top-notch legal experts for his defense team, a former district attorney named Luke Baker, and a former judge named Barnett. But District Attorney Kell was also feeling optimistic and told reporters that he was confident that Hugh Smith would be convicted. Two more arrests had been made in the case, one of them was Smith's brother, Sam, and the other was a cousin. Kell hinted that Sam Smith was the accomplice mentioned by Elias Snyder.

It was also reported that a prayer meeting had been held in the home of Hugh's brother on the night of the fire and the girl's disappearance. In attendance were most of the Smith family and a family servant, a boy by the name of Jerome Valentine. Hugh Smith was suspiciously absent from the event. Sam Smith left the house immediately after the meeting was over, consistent with the time of the sawmill fire.

Local opinion over Hugh Smith's innocence was divided, but few thought that Hugh would hang for the crime of which he was accused. Too many years had gone by, and too many valuable witnesses had passed away. Those who were left were too old and too absent-minded to remember facts and details.

Others insisted that old Hugh Smith, with his largeness of heart, his extraordinary kindness, and his naturally sympathetic disposition, could not have possibly killed the harmless, feeble-minded young woman known to locals as "Crazy Lindy."

Still, others recalled the strange behavior of Malinda's father after the girl's disappearance. On the Snyder property was a well that provided an abundance of clear, clean water. For some unknown reason, Mr. Snyder filled in the well and dug another not long after his daughter disappeared. Curiosity seekers and amateur sleuths had searched Smith's property—right down to his manure pile—for some shred of evidence that would put the noose around Smith's neck, but they found nothing. Everything hinged on the story of Elias Snyder.

Those who believed that Hugh Smith was innocent questioned Snyder's motives. It was known that one of Hugh's cousins, John Schull, had been suspected of the crime back when Malinda first disappeared, and that this cousin was a bitter enemy of Hugh Smith. It was rumored that this cousin also had "dirt" of an unrelated nature on Elias Snyder, and coerced

Snyder into fingering Hugh. Schull, who was now 73 years old, claimed that Malinda's body was first buried under a pile of leaves on the mountainside behind Hugh's home.

There was a disturbing sense that both Hugh and Sam Smith knew more about Malinda's death than they were letting on. One witness claimed that he had once heard Sam Smith brag to his wife that he "knew where the hatchet was that killed Lindy Snyder." Sam Smith's wife, however, was long dead and, therefore, could not corroborate this claim.

Then, a few days after the arrest of Hugh and Sam Smith, Jerome Valentine came forward and told authorities that once, when he was a "bound boy" working for the Smith family, Hugh had threatened to kill him if he ever told anybody about something that had happened on the property. Valentine didn't understand what Hugh was referring to at the time but believed that it might have been the murder.

Other witnesses came forward who recalled that Hugh's first wife, on her deathbed, claimed that she had a statement to make before she passed away. According to witnesses, Hugh shooed them all away from his wife's bedside before she could make her deathbed confession.

On March 26, 1897, Hugh Smith was taken into court on a writ of habeas corpus. After the district attorney failed to provide the judge with any tangible evidence connecting Smith to the supposed murder of Malinda Snyder, the accused killer was set free by Judge Lyons. The only thing that anyone could prove beyond a doubt was that Malinda had disappeared. There was no body, no murder weapon, no physical evidence whatsoever.

It is still open to debate whether Hugh Smith, with the help of his brother, murdered "Crazy Lindy," cut up her body, and cremated the remains in the fireplace of an abandoned farmhouse in Liberty Valley. But, if Hugh Smith did manage to get away with murder, his triumph was short-lived. He died of natural causes on September 16, 1898.

15.

DEBUNKING THE GHOSTS OF AMITY HALL

(PERRY COUNTY)

The historic tavern known as Amity Hall, near the confluence of the Juniata and Susquehanna rivers, is arguably the most famous haunted place in Perry County. Built in 1810, the tavern operated continuously until it was set ablaze by a careless amateur ghost hunter in 2009, except for a thirty-year period when it was used as a private residence. Today, the burned-out ruins can still be seen behind a barbed-wire fence just off the Amity Hall exit of Route 322.

During its heyday in the era of canal boats and stagecoaches, Amity Hall was one of the most famous taverns in Pennsylvania, and remained so well into the 20th century, due to its ideal location at the intersection of the Susquehanna Trail (Route 15) and the William Penn Highway (Rt. 322).

According to tradition, famous guests have included inventor Thomas Edison, poet Edwin Markham, and boxer Jack Dempsey. Charles Dickens was also said to have stayed there, but since that is a claim made by the owners of virtually every historic tavern in America, one should probably take that claim with a grain of salt. Nonetheless, Amity Hall has offered food and lodging to generations of hungry and weary travelers from all corners of the globe, famous or otherwise.

THE EARLY YEARS

The charred remains of Amity Hall sit on a parcel of land that was once known as Huling's Ordinary, which was owned by early settler Marcus Huling, and used as a rest stop by travelers along the old post road. A small tavern was constructed on the site in 1744. The Huling family operated it until the construction of the Philadelphia-Pittsburgh turnpike, which brought such a large volume of stagecoach traffic through the area that Huling decided to build the large, commodious 23-room Amity Hall, which was billed as "the friendly inn."

When railroads supplanted stagecoaches after the Civil War, travel time was reduced dramatically, and, as a result, business declined for many inns and taverns. Amity Hall was no exception. In 1892 the building was purchased by Dr. George Nutz Reutter, whose family used Amity Hall as a private residence until 1922.

Three generations of the Reutter family lived—and died—on the estate, dating back to 1830 when Dr. Daniel Nelson Ludwig Reutter occupied the grounds formerly known as Huling's Ordinary during the construction of the Pennsylvania Canal. After he died in 1846, he was laid to rest on the grounds. Amity Hall was eventually sold by the widow of Dr. Harry D. Reutter in the 1920s and, thanks to the advent of the automobile, once again became a popular hostelry.

The bodies of deceased members of the Reutter family were removed from the Amity Hall family plot in October of 1927 and re-buried at the Presbyterian Cemetery in Duncannon. History records the following names as members of the Reutter family who died and were buried at Amity Hall: Daniel Nelson Ludwig Reutter (1800-1846), Mary Jane Re-utter (1838-1839), Wilson Hazlet Reutter (1841-1842), Imogene Reutter (1842-1842), Thomas Hood Reutter (1836-1863), Ida Grace Reutter

(1865-1867), Margaret Imogene Reutter (1868-1869), Margaret Smith Reutter (1835-1879), and George Nutz Reutter (1836-1890).

Since five of these burials were of infants and children, perhaps it is no surprise that Amity Hall developed a spooky reputation over the years. Even the adults who lived at Amity Hall had short lifespans, even by 19th-century standards.

REBIRTH OF THE TAVERN

W.B. "Billy" Brown, who, along with business partner H.Z. Arney, purchased Amity Hall from Reutter's widow, firmly believed in preserving the historic charm of the red brick building and filled its 23 rooms with early American antique furniture. As automobile travel grew in popularity, Brown grew Amity Hall into one of the finest tourist stops in Pennsylvania. By the 1930s, Amity Hall boasted a lunch counter as well as a full restaurant, beer gardens, a truck stop, miniature golf, barbershop, and even in a drive-in movie theatre. In May of 1922, while renovating the property for the tavern's re-opening, workers found dozens of curious relics secreted beneath floorboards and inside the walls of the structure, including Indian arrowheads and a book printed in 1833.

HAUNTED OR NOT?

In May of 2009, the Amity Hall complex was destroyed by a fire set by ghost hunters. Only the brick walls from the original tavern escaped destruction. A construction company from Steelton demolished the complex in December of 2014 and erected a chain-link fence around the ruins of the tavern. While it is always tragic to see a building of historical significance destroyed by reckless trespassers, the irony is that many ghost stories associated with Amity Hall are complete nonsense with no basis in historical fact.

One such claim appearing on a popular website of haunted places states:

Although the Amity Hall burned to the ground in the late 2000s, it was alleged to be extremely active with the haunts. A man was said to have killed his wife by stabbing her on the porch sofa, then killed his children and himself upstairs. Apparitions, black figures, and flashes of light have been spotted, and some witnesses claim to have seen reenactments of the grisly murder.

There is, of course, no historical record of any such incident taking place. However, these rumors may have stemmed from a 1965 triple homicide that took place on North High Street in Duncannon, when a Sunday school teacher by the name of Byron Halter murdered his daughter, wife, and mother-in-law then committed suicide in Northumberland County after fleeing from the police.

Another popular claim about the supposed ghosts of Amity Hall states that the tavern was used as a military hospital during the Civil War. This claim can easily be disproved, as there were no Civil War battles fought in Perry County, and Gettysburg is over fifty miles away.

Perhaps the only spooky thing about Amity Hall is that it was once the site of the Reutter family graveyard, where numerous children were buried. But it may disappoint some ghost hunters to learn that none of these children were murdered, and those who drew their final breaths at Amity Hall all passed away from either illness or natural causes. Sadly, if only those amateur paranormal investigators had done their research, the historically important tavern might still be welcoming weary travelers today.

16.

THE DEATHBED CONFESSION OF HETTY GOOD

(LANCASTER COUNTY)

W hen a sweet, old Mennonite woman from Bowmansville saw death standing on her doorstep after a long bout with tuberculosis, she attempted to end her life by slashing her throat. Her suicide attempt was a failure, however, and as she lay in bed waiting for the dreaded disease to succeed where her frail hands and razor blade had failed, she called not for a priest, but for a former lover she hadn't seen in over forty years. With her dying breath, she made a ghastly confession—that she was one of the most ruthless, cold-blooded murderers Lancaster County had ever seen.

Hetty Good confessed her bone-chilling crimes on June 7, 1895, at the age of 61. A week earlier, perhaps overcome by guilt, she had attempted to cut her own throat, but only succeeded in prolonging her anguish for a few more days. Knowing that the end was rapidly approaching, she sent for a man from Mohnsville named William Griffiths, who formerly lived in Bowmansville.

William had been Hetty's lover four decades earlier, as was said to have been the father of Hetty Good's illegitimate child who had mysteriously disappeared from home one day, never to be seen again. At the time, it was believed that the baby had been kidnapped by gypsies or perhaps had wandered away when her mother's back was turned. At any rate, suspicion never fell upon Hetty or William, who eventually decided to sever their relationship and go their separate ways.

Griffiths must have been perplexed, if not outright stunned, when he received Hetty's request, but he immediately traveled from Berks County to Lancaster County to be at the bedside of his dying former lover. But what ensued was not a tearful reunion, but a sickening revelation—Hetty confessed that she had beaten out their baby's brains and buried the body in the yard of her house.

After sending Griffiths away, Hetty then sent for a Mennonite preacher, Rev. John Horning, of Bowmansville. The additional crime she confessed to Rev. Horning was equally horrendous.

Hetty told the preacher that she had also poisoned her grandmother, Mrs. Hutchinson, several years earlier. Hetty said that she had done the deed with the full consent of her grandfather, Mr. Hutchinson, who passed away not long afterward. Mrs. Hutchinson was sickly and decrepit, and both Hetty and her grandfather believed that they would be doing her a favor by putting her out of her misery (Mrs. Hutchinson might have said otherwise if she had been asked, however).

After making her confession to Rev. Horning, Hetty Good slipped into a deep, troubled sleep and passed away. But the strange story does not end there.

Once word spread that the sweet old lady from Bowmansville had slaughtered her baby and poisoned her grandmother, neighbors recalled that Hetty's mother had also passed away under mysterious circumstances.

Two years earlier, Hetty and her mother had shared a home, and neighbors remembered the way that Hetty used to complain about having to support her frail, elderly mother. One day, Mrs. Good suddenly became ill, and Hetty turned away all visitors. The nature of Mrs. Good's illness was a mystery, as doctors were not permitted to see her. Mrs. Good's condition worsened, and she soon died.

Although she never confessed to killing her mother, many residents of Bowmansville believed that Hetty Good was responsible for the deaths of her child, mother, and grandmother. If such was the case, then Hetty Good was not only one of the most heartless killers Pennsylvania has ever known, but also one of the most successful, since she reached the end of her life without ever having been suspected of committing any crimes.

17.

THE LOVE CULT MURDER

(LUZERNE COUNTY)

One of the most peculiar crimes in the history of northeastern Pennsylvania occurred in 1931 with the slaying of a reclusive elderly spinster from Forty Fort named Minnie Dilley. While most murders in our state's history have carried out by drunken thugs, heartless outlaws, and seasoned criminals, Miss Dilley's slayer was a young female college graduate and the daughter of an ordained minister. Stranger still, the unfortunate elderly victim was alleged by her deranged killer to have belonged to a bizarre sex cult.

A media sensation was created on Wednesday, April 8, when a beautiful 29-year-old woman named Frances Thomsen confessed to the brutal bludgeoning and attempted decapitation of Minnie Dilley, a well-to-do 76-year-old spinster from Luzerne County. The confessed killer, who graduated from the prestigious halls of Wellesley College, was the mother of three young children and a beloved schoolteacher adored by her pupils and colleagues. She had once lived across the street from the victim.

Minnie Dilley

But what strange series of events had led to this heinous, ghastly crime?

Frances Thomsen confessed that she had killed Minnie Dilley on the morning of Friday, April 3, 1931, between the hours of eight and nine o'clock. On the orders of Luzerne County District Attorney Thomas M. Lewis, Thomsen was brought back to city hall in Wilkes-Barre but, although the schoolteacher had been happy to confess, she adamantly refused to reveal a motive for the stunningly brutal and inexplicable crime.

Anning Dilley, the spinster's nephew, discovered Minnie's body in front of a fireplace inside her sprawling River Street home in Forty Fort on April 4 after his knock on the door went unanswered. According to police, the victim's head had been beaten viciously beyond recognition, and the head was nearly severed from the torso. A filled bottle of ginger ale was found on the floor, and it was believed by investigators the glass bottle had been used to bludgeon the old woman in the head. The weapon used to slice open her throat was not found.

Dilley was rumored to be an heiress to a large fortune, and police immediately suspected that the motive for the crime was financial gain, even though there was no evidence of a robbery. Miss Dilley lived in a large, luxurious home at 98 River Street and owned many valuable possessions, but not one thing was missing. Police examined her diary for a possible clue but lost hope after discovering that Minnie's most recent journal entry had been made in 1921.

The Dilley name was one of the oldest and most respected in the Wyoming Valley, and within hours word of the murder spread throughout the country; news of the crime made the front pages of newspapers as far away as Albuquerque and El Paso. The Dilleys arrived in Wyoming Valley from Cape May, New Jersey, in 1784. The Rolling Mill Hill section of Wilkes-Barre was named for the large mill owned by Minnie's grandfather, Jesse Dilley. Other family members became prominent civic leaders. Because of the prestige associated with the family name, the Dilley murder was discussed from coast to coast.

Meanwhile, back in Luzerne County, wild rumors were running rampant.

Miss Dilley was said to be quite eccentric, and she also prided herself in being an amateur architect. Like the famous Winchester House in San Jose, Dilley's home featured an assortment of architectural oddities; each room in the three-story stucco house contained two doors, one which opened inwardly, while the other opened in the opposite direction. One room that overlooked the Susquehanna River featured unique v-shaped windows. And, much like the equally eccentric recluse Sarah Winchester, Minnie Dilley always kept her home in a state of continual construction.

The local paper, the *Wilkes-Barre Times Leader*, was quick to print any rumors about the murder. On April 6, the newspaper claimed that the killer was known and that his identity would be revealed in a short time (County Detective Richard Powell and State Police Captain William A. Clark dismissed this claim, however). It was also reported that a threatening letter was found in one of the victim's pockets (this, too, was denied by police). When asked for a statement, the victim's nephew, Anning Dilley, mocked the *Times Leader* for its reckless reporting. He quipped, "You people know more about me than I do."

The Dilley murder must have been exhausting for local reporters; even the victim's closest relatives confessed to knowing little about her private life. "If everyone knew her as we did, they know nothing about her," one relative remarked.

On Tuesday, April 7, local papers claimed that authorities had identified Dilley's killer and promised that an arrest would be made before nightfall. Captain Clark of the State Police told reporters that they now believed revenge to be the motive, and that the spinster's killer might have been a woman, and that the suspect's every move was under surveillance. The entire Wyoming Valley sat on the edge of their seats in anticipation of further developments.

The following evening Carl Thomsen, a salesman for a lumber company, sat at his kitchen table in Pittsburgh, motionless, with a dazed expression on his face, upon learning that his estranged wife had been arrested. Officers hauled his wife down to police headquarters for questioning after finding her wandering the streets of the city. She had left him on Wednesday, leaving behind a note saying not to worry. By the time he had regained his composure, dressed, and made his way to the police station, his wife was already en route to Wilkes-Barre, in the custody of Assistant District Attorney Coughlin and County Detective Dempsey.

A large crowd of the curious were on hand in Luzerne County to welcome Frances Thomsen back to the place where she and her husband had called home four years earlier. She was described as small, slightly built, and extremely attractive by those who watched her being whisked out of the automobile and into police headquarters. She had protested her innocence throughout the long drive and claimed that the elderly spinster had held a "mysterious influence" over her husband.

Inside the police station, Thomsen was unable to provide an alibi, and gave rambling, conflicting stories regarding her whereabouts on the day of the murder. Police were convinced that Mrs. Thomsen was mentally unbalanced, and it was later reported that the former Latimer Junior High English teacher was known to have suffered from hallucinations. According to Frances, she had disappeared after learning that her husband was planning on placing her into a mental institution. Carl Thomsen later denied this claim.

During her grilling at police headquarters, she initially denied killing the wealthy recluse. She did, however, make some interesting statements.

Frances also told Coughlin a wild story—that Minnie Dilley wanted Carl Thomsen to preside over a "love cult" composed of schoolteachers. She then said to Coughlin, "If they put me in the electric chair, it certainly will be a joke." The assistant district attorney asked her what she meant. "Perhaps I should say, rather, it would be a travesty," she remarked.

Meanwhile, detectives in Allegheny County searched the Thomsen home and found several bottles of ginger ale. For Frances Thomsen, the jig was up. She admitted that she had hitch-hiked from Pittsburgh to Luzerne County to kill Miss Dilley, bashing her over the head with a bottle and then slashing her throat with a bread knife she had concealed inside her umbrella. She then hitch-hiked back to Pittsburgh. "I did it in self-defense," she insisted. "It was her life or mine!"

The following day, Assistant D.A. Coughlin announced that Frances Thomsen would probably be turned over to the Lunacy Commission. Judge McLean, on the other hand, wasn't as convinced that the killer was insane.

On Saturday, April 11, Frances made her first court appearance. She was represented by a well-known lawyer, John Dando, who had been hired by the Wellesley Alumni Association. Louise McBride, one of the country's leading female attorneys, had also been retained by the alumni association.

During the hearing, some interesting evidence was produced; District Attorney Thomas M. Lewis entered into evidence several letters Thomsen had written to Dilley. In these letters, Thomsen had accused the spinster of attempting to form a "love cult" and using her "unholy witch powers" to steal away her husband. In these letters, Frances accused Minnie of making plans to establish a secret sex colony in the Poconos—a claim she made again on the witness stand. "I am in great danger by saying this because it involves a great many people in Forty Fort," declared the killer. "They plan to establish a love cult with my husband as the presiding head, for teachers and business girls who cannot afford to live a married life."

Frances smiled as Assistant District Attorney Coughlin read from another letter, dated March 5, 1929, written to Minnie Dilley's brother,

Sherman. "Your sister, Miss Dilley, is and has been for years breaking up my home. She has tempted my husband with money. She has a strange, unholy power over him. She would build a bungalow for him, and she'd take the children, if she couldn't have him alone."

When questioned about the murder, Frances admitted to it, but still maintained that it was in self-defense. Nonetheless, she was charged with first-degree murder. After the arraignment, she was embraced by her teary-eyed husband. "Oh, dear Frances," he sobbed. "I'm so sorry."

Frances smiled as though she did not comprehend the seriousness of what was happening. She patted her husband on the head, saying, "Don't worry, Carl. Everything will be alright in a short time."

Carl, of course, denied knowing anything about this bizarre "love cult." During the preliminary hearing, he testified that the claims were the result of his wife's "jealously insane mind."

"She often accused me of cooperating with Miss Dilley in a plan to start a 'school for love' in the Poconos, and sometimes she imagined we were going to establish it in the heart of New York City," he testified. "The very idea is absurd. Miss Dilley never even intimated such a thing to me."

He also explained that his wife claimed to have gotten these messages "from the air," and that she believed she possessed a power to receive these messages like "some sort of radio machine."

But things were looking quite grim indeed; although numerous witnesses—including her Baptist minister father and several former Wellesley classmates—testified that Frances was not mentally fit to stand trial, Judge McLean still decided to charge the ex-teacher with first-degree murder, even though John Dando argued that his client would not have a fair trial because the Dilleys had many powerful and influential friends in the community.

Louise McBride also shared this concern, instructing Dando to spare no expense in defending Thomsen. Dando also received a telegraph from Ira D. Farquarhar, a famous criminal defense attorney in Boston who had been eagerly following the case. Farquarhar believed that Thomsen was certifiably insane and offered to join the defense team.

MRS. FRANCES THOMSEN, 29, (left) Wellesley graduate and mother of three children, is held at Wilkes-Barre, Penn., on a charge of killing Miss Minnie Dilley, 76, (right) wealthy spinster. Authorities ascribed the murder to Mrs. Thomsen's belief that the aged spinster had exercised an "influence" over her husband, Carl Thomsen, and because she feared a "love cult" which, it is alleged, the slain woman wished to establish with Thomsen's aid.

There is another remarkable incident connected with the arraignment of Frances Thomsen. There was such a large crowd of gawkers and reporters at the courthouse that officials were forced to devise a novel method for delivering Miss Dilley's killer to Judge McLean's courtroom on the third floor without obstruction. Frances was lifted through the ground floor window by Detective Dempsey, who then walked her around the building to a little-used basement entrance. She was whisked onto an elevator in the basement and delivered to the third floor. According to Dempsey, the young woman was highly amused by this treatment.

On Monday, April 20, while Frances awaited her trial behind bars, Luzerne County Warden William B. Healey presented a petition to Judge McLean asking for the appointment of a sanity commission. In his letter, the warden insisted that Frances Thomsen was mentally ill and required urgent institutional care. Typically, filing such a petition would have been the responsibility of John Dando, but the defense attorney had fallen seriously ill while in Philadelphia. Nothing more could be done until Dando recovered from his illness, and so national attention turned away from the murder trial and turned towards Miss Dilley's will. More than a handful of people were immensely curious about whether the aged spinster had bequeathed a large sum of money for the establishment of a sex colony in the Pocono Mountains.

Others simply wanted to get their hands on the Dilley fortune. From Montana to California, people claiming to be distant relatives of Minnie Dilley deluged Luzerne County authorities with letters. One such letter came from Mary Long of Kemmerer, Wyoming, who claimed that her uncle was Benjamin Dilley and, therefore, she was entitled to a share of the Dilley estate. This letter, like all the others, was turned over to the State Police. In almost every case, the alleged relative was proven to be a con artist.

On the afternoon of Thursday, April 23, Judge McLean reluctantly agreed to appoint a lunacy commission to investigate the mental health condition of Frances Thomsen. The three members of the board were Dr. George Baskett, of the Retreat State Hospital, Dr. Stanley Freeman, the physician at the county prison, and Joseph Fleitz, an attorney and former State Workman's Compensation Board member. They determined that Thomsen was indeed insane and ought to be institutionalized immediately before she could harm herself—or worse.

On May 1, she was committed by Judge McLean to the mental asylum at Retreat.

Two weeks later, the contents of Minnie Dilley's will were finally revealed. The will, made on May 22, 1924, and placed by the deceased in a safety deposit box at the Second National Bank in Forty Fort, sent shockwaves throughout the Wyoming Valley. Not because Dilley bequeathed part of her vast fortune to establish a sex colony (she didn't, of course), but because the eccentric spinster was not nearly as wealthy as everyone had believed. The bulk of her estate was valued at just $22,000, and much to the chagrin of would-be descendants across the country, Miss Dilley chose to leave almost every penny to charity.

And so ends the sad and remarkable tale of a legendary fortune that turned out to be a myth and a sex colony that turned out to be nothing more than the figment of a young woman's diseased imagination.

As for Frances Thomsen, she never made it out of the insane asylum at Retreat. Sadly, her health, both physical and mental, continued to deteriorate. She died in March of 1940 at the age of 41, her demise barely warranting a couple of sentences on the back pages of the Wilkes-Barre paper. According to the report of her death, which was published more than two weeks after it occurred, her parents came from Wisconsin to claim the body, which rests at Oakwood Cemetery in Dodge County alongside her husband, Carl, who passed away in 1951 after his car was struck by a train at a railroad crossing in Waverly, New York.

18.

RED NOSE MIKE

(LUZERNE COUNTY)

I f a Hall of Fame existed for Pennsylvania criminals, 19th-century outlaw Red Nose Mike would have gotten inducted on the first ballot with the greatest of ease. After he was hanged in 1889, the blood-thirsty killer with the curious nickname became part of Luzerne County legend. A great deal has been written about Red Nose Mike over the years—much of it true, but some of it grossly exaggerated, and these exaggerations only served to spread his infamy and reputation throughout every corner of the state. Here is the true story of Michael Rizzolo, the heartless bandit known as Red Nose Mike.

Rizzolo, who earned his colorful sobriquet because of the unusual protrusion and color of his nose, was operating a commissary near Laurel Run when the Lehigh Valley Railroad was constructing its cutoff over the mountains from Coxton to Mountaintop. The contractor in charge of the cutoff construction was a man by the name of Charles McFadden, who employed many workers.

October 19, 1888, was payday for McFadden's employees. As usual, paymaster J.B. "Barney" McClure and his bodyguard, Hugh Flanagan, went to the Wyoming National Bank to obtain their workers' salaries, in this case, $12,000. Before they were able to make it back to the job site, McClure and Flanagan were gunned down in cold blood and robbed, their bodies and horse sprawled lifeless across a lonely road four miles from Wilkes-Barre. Both men had been ambushed from behind and had been killed instantly.

It was Charles McFadden who discovered the bodies not far from the job site. He returned in a panic to headquarters and notified the authorities and instructed his bosses to place the bodies of the murdered men in a wagon and transport them to the undertaker in Miner's Mills.

After two hunters near the scene of the crime had been arrested, Justice Coxe of Parsons determined that they had nothing to do with the murder and the men were released, but not before informing the authorities that the likely culprit may have been at Thomas Quigley's saloon in Miner's Mills. The morning of the murder had been wet and cold, and work on the job site had been suspended. On that morning, several Italian railroad laborers had left their shanties and gone to Quigley's saloon to get an early start on their daily consumption of liquor. Detectives later went to the saloon to pursue this lead.

They learned that on the morning of the murder—about 35 minutes before the killings took place—four Italians left the saloon and started up the mountain to their shanties. One Italian, Red Nose Mike, remained at the saloon. Witnesses recalled that he seemed fidgety; every few minutes, he would get up and peek out the window. About ten minutes later, he left the tavern. A few minutes later, McClure and Flanagan arrived at the saloon to purchase cigars. Quigley asked them to stay, but McClure said that they had to be getting along because the workers were expecting their pay. That was the last time the two men were seen alive.

Although Red Nose Mike was a suspect from the start, his close ties with local law enforcement and local judges afforded him a measure of protection; they were reluctant to question him and hesitant to take any action. Pinkerton agents, who had been tailing Rizzolo, declined to make an arrest. One local detective, identified only as Roberts, did manage to arrest Red Nose Mike, but the magistrate at Miners Mills, Squire Moore, ordered his release. Quigley had served as Mike's legal counsel during the proceeding.

But Charles McFadden had a plan; he transferred Red Nose Mike to a job site in Poughkeepsie and hired four Pinkerton detectives to keep him under surveillance. If the police and magistrates of northeastern Pennsylvania were unwilling to bring Rizzolo to justice, perhaps law enforcement in another state would be able to get the job done.

["RED NOSE MIKE."]

Two of the detectives, disguised as immigrant laborers, lodged with Rizzolo in Stamfordsville, near Poughkeepsie, and soon noticed that he had begun spending money freely. He bought several Christmas presents and shipped them to his friends and relatives in Italy. He began to dress extravagantly and had a habit of purchasing expensive wine by the case. When one of the undercover Pinkerton agents asked Red Nose Mike about his wild spending, he told him that a rich uncle from Italy had died and left him his fortune.

One night, shortly after Christmas, one of the detectives, Frank Thayer, saw Mike remove a large roll of bills from his trunk. The detective ripped off his disguise and placed the suspect under arrest. He was then taken to Philadelphia, where, in the presence of Captain Linden of the Philadelphia Pinkerton office, he made a full confession.

THE CONFESSION OF RED NOSE MIKE

"I was the leader of five Italians. We concocted the murder. I had plenty of money, but my friends had not. Early on the morning of October 19 last, we left our shanties and came to Wilkes-Barre, arriving at 10:30. I told my comrades to go up the mountain and wait. I timed McClure and knew when he was due. I started ahead of him and waited for him at the knoll on the hill. When he came into view, I gave the signal to the other men; they fired, and the work was done. Winchester rifles were used. McClure's horse started to run away but was shot from the rear and brought to a halt. At one time, there was great danger of the horse running away, taking with him in the buggy the money. We buried the guns near the scene of the murder and took the money to our shanty and secreted it."

Red Nose Mike implicated four of his friends in the murder; Joseph and Antino Bevevino, Vincenzo Vellali, and Pedrio Lumechi. Lumechi, who had once been a sharpshooter in the Italian army, was the one who pulled the trigger. They managed to evade capture and fled the country. A Pinkerton detective from London eventually tracked them down in Mida, Italy.

District Attorney Darte of Luzerne County and Captain Linden presented their evidence to Secretary of State Thomas F. Bayard, who sent extradition papers to Italy. The Italian government, however, refused to surrender the wanted men. When James Blaine became the Secretary of State in 1889, he decided to let the matter rest so as not to cause a rift between the United States and Italy, much to Captain Linden's chagrin.

Two of Rizzolo's accomplices, Vellali and Bevevino, were eventually tried and convicted in an Italian court for their role in the murders of McClure and Flanagan. In 1894 they were both sentenced to twenty years in prison. Interestingly, though Vellali, Lumechi and the Bevevino brothers had played a far more significant role in the deadly ambush than Rizzolo, Red Nose Mike was the only one who would pay for the crime with his life.

RED NOSE MIKE SWINGS INTO ETERNITY

A grand jury indicted Rizzolo on January 11, 1889, and his case went to trial on February 7. On February 11, he was found guilty of murder in the first degree and sentenced to death by hanging. On June 22, Sheriff Search entered Mike's cell and read the death warrant to him; he was scheduled to hang the following Tuesday. The condemned man didn't flinch as the warrant was read. He waited until the sheriff was done reading, then said, simply, "Alright, sir."

The city was brimming with excitement over the impending execution. Sheriff Search was besieged with requests for tickets to the hanging, but under the law, only two dozen witnesses would be granted admittance to the jail yard.

The weather was beautiful on the morning of June 30, 1889, but it seemed that every shopkeeper in Wilkes-Barre had closed his doors early in anticipation of a slow business day. Before the sun had fully risen, hundreds had flocked to the prison, and hundreds more ascended hills and climbed to rooftops, hoping to gain a vantage point that would allow them a peek into the jail yard.

Shortly after 9 o'clock, Red Nose Mike's spiritual advisors visited him in his cell. Meanwhile, Warden Brockway ordered the gates open, and there was a mad rush for the jail yard. The guards scrutinized tickets, and it was discovered that numerous forgeries were in the hands of morbid curiosity seekers. But even the excitement of legitimate ticketholders faded to somber silence when their eyes fell upon the dreaded gallows.

Red Nose Mike displayed steely resolve as he was led to the platform, giving no impression of fear, remorse, or sadness. He showed no emotion at all as the black cap was placed over his head, and his arms pinioned behind his back, and the efficient hangman, Atkinson, finished his task so quickly that those who blinked might have missed it.

It was 10:16 when his body fell, but his neck was not broken. It took fifty-three minutes before he died of strangulation. His body was cut down and turned over to Undertaker Peter Conniff and his assistants, who had arrived through a rear entrance. The body of Red Nose Mike was lowered into an imitation rosewood coffin and conveyed to St. Mary's Cemetery in Hanover Township.

There is a strange post-script in the story of Red Nose Mike, however.

On February 21, 1892, it was discovered that someone had stolen the body of Red Nose Mike from the cemetery. A week earlier, two men from Wilkes-Barre were sitting in a saloon reminiscing about the outlaw, when one proposed a drunken wager. "Fifteen bucks says Mike's body isn't really in the grave where it was said to have been placed," said one of the men. The wager was accepted, and a "colored man named Packer" was hired to open the grave. Cloaked by the darkness of night and obscured by the pounding of rain, the gravedigger went to work. When the coffin was opened, Packer discovered that there was nothing inside. He was so shocked that he fled from the scene without filling the grave back in, and the two men who had made the bet were compelled to procure shovels and finish Packer's job.

So, whatever happened to the body of Red Nose Mike? There are a few possible explanations, though there is nobody alive who knows for sure. One possibility is that his body was stolen and sold to a medical school for dissection since body snatching was not uncommon during this time. But since Red Nose Mike was buried in a pauper's unmarked grave, it's also possible that Packer—who was digging at night in a steady rain—had simply opened the wrong grave by mistake. Perhaps someday, a brittle scrap of paper from the 19th century or the discovery of a long-forgotten diary will solve the mystery. But, until then, all we can do is wonder.

19.

THE EXECUTION OF MICHAEL ROSEBERRY

(LUZERNE COUNTY)

D ozens of criminals have expiated their crimes on the gallows of Luzerne County. Still, very little is known about Michael Roseberry, who holds the distinction of being the first person executed in Luzerne County. But what makes the story of Roseberry's execution in 1779 remarkable is that it was not carried out under state law, but federal military law.

At the beginning of the American Revolution, both British and American forces sought allegiances with the Six Nations of the powerful Iroquois Confederacy. The Mohawk, Cayuga, Seneca, and Onandaga nations ultimately sided with the British, while the Oneida and Tuscarora allied themselves with the American revolutionaries. By June of 1778, it seemed inevitable that a major war involving the now-divided Iroquois would soon break out, and the Continental Congress called for a military expedition (led by General Horatio Gates) that would serve as an unexpected "first strike" against the Seneca.

However, the British had also been plotting their own first strike, which transpired before the Gates Expedition could get underway. On July 3, 1778, British Loyalist John Butler led his militia, known as Butler's Rangers, and a party of Iroquois warriors into the Wyoming Valley (which, at the time, was part of Connecticut) and decimated the Continental forces of Zebulon Butler. The battle was brief and bloody, lasting less than an hour, but when the smoke cleared, 340 of Zebulon Butler's 360 men were dead; the rest were captured. Only one of Butler's Rangers were killed, along with one Indian. The Iroquois took 227 scalps that day, and over one thousand homes were burned to the ground.

To add a morbid exclamation point to the appalling carnage, the Iroquois tortured and killed the few dozen survivors who had surrendered, leaving their unburied bodies to rot in the hot summer sun. It wasn't until October 22 that the fallen patriots were properly laid to rest when a detail led by Lieutenant John Jenkins gathered the bare bones and buried them in a mass grave. In 1832, the city of Wilkes-Barre erected a monument on the site of the mass grave.

According to several corroborating stories told by survivors who managed to flee to Delaware after the Battle of Wyoming, the prisoners of war captured by the Iroquois were stood in rows on the order of Esther Montour, otherwise known as Queen Esther, who became the leader of the tribe after the death of her husband, Echogohund. It was on a large outcropping of rock near Forty Fort, known locally as Bloody Rock, that Queen Esther bashed in the heads of the prisoners, one by one, with a war club.

The following summer, General George Washington retaliated by launching the Sullivan Expedition, led by Major General John Sullivan of New Hampshire. Sullivan's order was to show no mercy, and the Continental Army's scorched earth campaign resulted in the destruction of 40 Iroquois villages in upstate New York. Sullivan was so hungry for revenge that he ordered his men to slaughter any horse that could not keep up the pace during the army's 450-mile journey from Easton to Elmira. In September of 1779, when the expedition reached Chemung County, Sullivan ordered the slaughter of dozens of his exhausted horses, and local Indians later collected the skulls and lined them up along the trail, thereby giving the town in Chemung County its peculiar name—Horseheads, New York.

One of the enlisted men who took part in the Sullivan Expedition was a soldier by the name of Michael Roseberry. Although records are scarce, it seems likely that Roseberry was part of the expeditionary force which departed from Easton, Northampton County, on June 18, 1779. Proof of this comes from cemetery records; of the hundreds of Roseberrys buried in Pennsylvania, more than half are buried in and around Easton, while none are from the Wyoming Valley. Therefore, it stands to reason that Roseberry was a native of Northampton County.

From Easton, the main army, numbering 3,500 men, marched for five days to an encampment in Luzerne County, known as the Bullock farm, arriving on June 23. Sullivan's army remained in Luzerne County for over a month awaiting fresh supplies and provisions.

It was during this month-long delay that some of the men began to lose heart and desert Sullivan's army. Upon investigation, it was learned that two men had been responsible for instigating the wave of desertions— Lawrence Miller and Michael Roseberry. Both men were condemned to death by court-martial after a trial in Wilkes-Barre, and Roseberry was hanged on July 1, 1779, on a gallows erected along the riverbank.

As for Lawrence Miller, he showed a great deal of remorse for his actions, and his wife and children appealed to the military judges to spare his life. Unfortunately, there was nobody to speak up for young Michael Roseberry. Just minutes after Roseberry had been hanged, right when the executioner was adjusting the noose around Miller's neck, General Sullivan himself arrived on horseback and announced a pardon. Records indicate that Miller returned to the ranks and remained a faithful soldier for the duration of the campaign.

Unfortunately, it remains unclear what happened to the body of Luzerne County's first victim of the gallows, Michael Roseberry. Was he laid to rest in an unmarked grave, like the tragic patriots of the Battle of Wyoming, somewhere along the banks of the Susquehanna? Or was his body claimed by relatives in Northampton County?

20.

THE MYSTERY BONES OF FEDERAL STREET

(LEBANON COUNTY)

When John Wentzel discovered a human skeleton buried in the basement of his Federal Street home in Lebanon in 1926, it set into motion a bizarre chain of events that whipped the entire city into a frenzy. It is a story of a chilling nightmare—following by a gruesome find—that still puzzles fans of unsolved paranormal mysteries to this day.

It all began in early December in 1926 when a 29-year-old man named John Wentzel began experiencing blood-chilling nightmares six years after moving into a home at 1149 Federal Street. Or, at least he thought they were nightmares—he couldn't be sure. Night after night, he was tormented by the face of a skeleton staring at him with angry, hollow eye sockets from the foot of his bed.

Perhaps even more chilling were the ominous words spoken by the disembodied phantom skull.

"The skeleton talked to me," Wentzel later told the police. "It said, 'Dig me out! Dig me out! I've been here for forty years, and I want to get out!'"

According to Wentzel, the ghostly visitations had frayed his nerves so much that his doctor, Dr. John L. Groh, had to prescribe medication. The nerve tonics helped for a while, but the medicine did not make the talking skull go away.

The phantom skull tormented Wentzel for several more days until he finally decided that he had to do something about it. Around noon on Saturday, December 4, he took a shovel and nervously went down into the cellar and began digging into the dirt floor, right where the midnight apparition had instructed him to dig. He hit paydirt with the very first strike of his shovel, in a spot located under the cellar stairs. Fifteen minutes later, after carefully digging around the buried object, he was staring at an oblong box containing mud-encrusted bones.

Wentzel immediately decided to report his find to the police, even though he was fully aware that they would not believe the story he was about to tell. He telephoned the chief of police, Harry Sealer, who rushed to the house along with Patrolman John Reed.

Of course, once word got out about the mystery skeleton, every newspaper reporter in Lebanon County made a pilgrimage to the house on Federal Street. Wentzel told reporters that he had often heard stories about the house being haunted. "I hear that someone was murdered here years ago," he told the *Lebanon Semi-Weekly News*, "and I guess it just sort of worked on my mind."

Meanwhile, Patrolman Reed diligently pursued every possible lead. He obtained property records and compiled reams of information on every family who had lived in the house. He interviewed neighbors and some of the oldest residents of the town, who told the officer that the Reformed cemetery had once been in the vicinity. However, nobody was old enough to recall just where the graveyard had been. Back then, the street was known as Cedar Avenue. Before that, during the 19th century, it was known as Strawberry Alley.

The prevailing theory was that Wentzel had unearthed the remains of someone whose grave had been overlooked when the old cemetery was relocated to a different part of the city many decades earlier.

But the skeleton told a different story; a six-inch metal file was found among the bones, suggesting that a murder might have taken place. The location of the bones in the basement also suggested a not-so-proper Christian burial. There was no top or bottom to the wooden box in which the remains were found, and the box had been buried just four inches beneath the surface.

On Monday morning, December 6, Coroner F. Allen Rutherford went to the Wentzel house to examine the bones. Because of the size of the jawbone and the condition of the teeth, the coroner believed that it was the skeleton of an adult female. However, the ribs, arms, legs, feet, and hands were inexplicably missing.

Suspicion immediately fell upon the discoverer of the bones, John Wentzel. It didn't help his case that local papers described the young man as "peculiar," with some reporters going so far as to suggest that Wentzel was a deranged lunatic. The *Lebanon Semi-Weekly News* wrote: "It may be learned that Wentzel is a psychopathic subject, or one who is suffering from a mental disorder."

A few days later, a former resident of 1147 Federal Street came forward with her own story, which made locals think twice about questioning Wentzel's sanity.

Mary Witman Snavely had grown up in the house and continued to live there for a few years after her marriage to William Snavely. She recalled an incident from her childhood when one morning she was startled by the sound of someone walking down the stairs. Her father was upstairs in bed at the time, and Mary was in the kitchen mixing batter for a pie. Knowing that it was long before her father's usual time to wake up, she approached the door to the stairs. As she opened the door, something that felt like a cold, clammy hand suddenly emerged from the darkness and touched her brow. She screamed and then fell into a dead faint, sending the mixing bowl into the air. The clatter awakened Mary's father. He rushed down the stairs and eventually revived her.

An hour after Mary told her story to the newspaper, and several hours before it appeared in print, John Wentzel told another reporter from the

Lebanon Daily News that the murder occurred on November 20, 1908. Wentzel couldn't explain why that date popped into his head.

Although Mary Witman Snavely and John Wentzel did not know each other personally and lived a considerable distance apart, it was soon learned that November 20, 1908, was the same day that Mary, then a young newlywed, had her eerie encounter on the stairs.

Amanda Witman, Mary's widowed mother, had lived at 1147 Federal Street for thirty years and stated that although she had never seen a ghost in that house, she had frequently heard doors slamming shut and felt strange winds blowing inside of closed rooms of the house. Wentzel's next-door neighbors stated they had heard chains rattling from inside the house at night and had seen and heard other strange things they could not explain.

Another widow by the name of Mrs. Maus had lived in the house for about ten years. She recalled that, many years earlier, a German family once lived there. One day the husband disappeared and was never seen or heard from again. According to Mrs. Maus, there were also many "houses of ill repute" located on Cedar Avenue during the late 1890s, and she believed that the skeleton was that of an unknown prostitute who had been illegally buried in the cellar of a brothel.

Although ghost fever was raging throughout Lebanon, not everyone who lived on Federal Street believed the spook stories. One such skeptic was a man by the name of Green, described by papers as a colored delicatessen merchant and pool room proprietor who lived across the street from Wentzel. When asked whether he believed in the ghost stories, Mr. Green replied, "I'm kept too busy watching the live ones to give a darn about the dead ones."

John Wentzel continued to have one problem, however; visitors from the spirit world were still tormenting him. He claimed to Dr. Rutherford during the coroner's inquest that on December 7 he had received a visit from a female entity, who told him that "Sam Moore was the man who done it," and that he believed the name of the victim was either Sarah Moore or Sarah Donmoyer. Wentzel said that the ghost told him the girl had been stabbed through the heart with the metal file. The apparition did not provide a motive or any other additional information, but Wentzel testified that the apparition was that of an attractive woman, who announced her presence by gripping him by the neck.

On the day of the inquest, another peculiar detail emerged, when it was recalled that a female's skeletal hand had been discovered a year and a half earlier. It was rescued from the mouth a dog, who had dug it up somewhere and carried it to a home on Federal Street. Patrolman Reed, intrigued by the coincidence, investigated the matter, but was unable to locate additional clues.

The following week, a new theory emerged about the mysterious skeleton of Federal Street after the coroner's report revealed that the bones had been buried north and south, unlike Christian burials, which are traditionally made with the feet to the east and the head to the west. Some speculated that the position of the skeleton indicated an Indian burial. Experts, however, quickly dismissed this idea.

Ultimately, it was concluded by authorities that the skeleton had been initially laid to rest in the old Reformed graveyard and had remained undisturbed until the construction of the home on Federal Street (then Cedar Avenue), when it was partially unearthed by workmen who, fearing the delays such an inconvenient find would inevitably create, worked "around" the corpse without telling anyone, covering it with a thin layer of dirt after the cellar had been excavated. This, the authorities claimed, would account for the missing top of the coffin.

The bones, according to newspaper accounts, were burned and the ashes scattered in an unspecified area.

As for the house that once stood at 1147 Federal Street, records indicate that it was torn down sometime in the late 1970s or early 1980s. Today, rows of nondescript apartments line the street, the tenants most likely unaware of the peculiar events that took place there in December of 1926. John Wentzel seems to have disappeared from history; some records suggest that Wentzel was not his real name (his father was an Italian immigrant, and it appears that Wentzel was the family's adopted American name), so whatever became of him is unknown.

But one cannot help but wonder just how he had gained his knowledge about the skeleton buried in his basement, and to whom that skeleton belonged. Perhaps supernatural forces were at play, and maybe the messages he claimed to have received from a ghostly skull and a beautiful female apparition really did hint at an unsolved murder that happened long, long ago.

DID JOHN WENTZEL SEE THE GHOST OF JOSIE MACKAY?

As stated earlier, Federal Street was known as Cedar Avenue in earlier times and was the site of many notorious brothels. During the coroner's inquest, Wentzel testified that he was regularly visited by the ghost of an attractive young woman who told him that the murder victim was named "Sarah Moore" or "Sarah Donmoyer." But if the ghostly visitor was not the murder victim, then whose ghost was seen by Wentzel? Evidence suggests that the spirit of the beautiful woman who appeared nightly to Wentzel may have been that of an unfortunate young prostitute named Josie Mackay who died of a self-inflicted gunshot wound in 1902, just a few feet away from the Wentzel house.

Josie Mackay was born in Lewistown and relocated to Cedar Avenue in Lebanon in the spring of 1902, working under the alias of "Goldie Croff." Shortly before one o'clock on the afternoon of May 24, she shot herself in the heart in an outbuilding at 1127 Cedar Avenue. Since the houses of the era were most likely row homes, it stands to reason that the location of this outbuilding was just a few steps from the Wentzel house.

Two rumors were surrounding Josie Mackay's death—one rumor maintained that she was a morphine addict, the other speculated that she had fallen in love with a man who later abandoned her, identified as Harry Welsh, a train conductor from Paxtang. The other girls who shared the house stated that as soon as Welsh took his leave, Josie took a revolver and went out into the back yard. Marie Harris, another girl who resided at the brothel, followed her into an outbuilding but became scared that Josie might turn the gun on her. She heard the gunshot before she reached the house and turned around just in time to see Josie staggering into the yard, where she collapsed.

Josie was rushed to the Good Samaritan Hospital. She did not lose consciousness after the shooting and was able to answer questions. She revealed that she had arrived in Lebanon from Harrisburg, where she had been in jail for shooting another woman. She had no parents or relatives but lived in the Cedar Avenue home with three other females and the madame of the establishment, Mrs. Sallie Burgner. After doctors removed the bullet from the 24-year-old woman's chest, her condition began to deteriorate. She died on May 30 and was buried at Mt. Lebanon Cemetery.

Could this have been the woman John Wenztel saw in the form of a ghost, telling him where to dig? In all probability, we may never know the answer to this chilling mystery.

21.

TRAGEDY ON THE SUSQUEHANNA

(NORTHUMBERLAND COUNTY)

Saturday morning, July 13, 1901, dawned sunny and bright, and the streets of Sunbury were buzzing with activity. While the women of the city made their weekly rounds to the shops and markets, the men and children headed to the river to fish and swim and make the most of this beautiful, lazy summer day.

At the Market Street wharf, where the Clements coal dredge and a few small wooden boats were moored, several boys were casting their lines into the water. Among them were Roy McDonald, age 11, Harry Reed, age 12, and William Pullen, 17. These boys were joined by two sets of brothers, Frank and Charles Keller, ages 8 and 12, and Arthur and Allen Fetzer, 11 and 14.

The boys were probably too preoccupied to pay much attention to the gathering of prominent Williamsport gentlemen who waited on the wharf with their poles and tackle boxes in hand. And they probably paid even less attention to Butler Wendt and William Gaughler, the engineers tinkering with the steam gauge of the Montour, a pleasure boat owned by the Sunbury Boat Club that was moored thirty-five feet away.

The Montour had just returned from Shamokin Dam earlier that morning, and Wendt and Gaughler were making the steamboat ready for its next excursion. Superintendent E.B. Westfall, of the Pennsylvania Railroad, had invited a party of railroad officials, bankers, lawyers, and other prominent businessmen out for a day of fishing on the Susquehanna. It was just after nine o'clock, and the engineers were almost done with their preparations.

Butler Wendt opened the fire door and threw in a few shovelfuls of coal. He then checked the steam gauge—it registered a perfect sixty-five pounds of steam. The water gauge indicated that the boiler was full. Satisfied that the Montour was ready to take Superintendent Westfall and his friends on their fishing trip, the engineers turned over the boat to her pilot, George Frymeyer, a veteran riverman who knew the Susquehanna better than anyone in Sunbury.

After his job was done, Wendt walked uptown to run some errands. By 9:45, he had nearly reached the Central Hotel, and that was when he heard what sounded like the blast of a mighty cannon. The explosion was so loud that everyone for miles around heard it. Women fled from the markets in fear, dropping their baskets of groceries to the ground. Some shouted that it was an earthquake. Others ran for cover, wondering if the quiet, rural countryside had been invaded by an unknown enemy army. When the initial shock subsided, it was evident that the explosion had come from the river, and several hundred residents of Sunbury raced to the wharf eager to discover what had happened.

The sight that met their searching eyes was far worse than anything they could have imagined.

One description of the tragedy, from the *Lewisburg Chronicle*, reads:

> Women turned pale and had to be helped away, and even robust men
> turned and left, so sad and pathetic was the scene.

One reporter from the *Williamsport Sun-Gazette* wrote sadly, but poetically:

> The scene was an awful one. Lying on the ground, writhing in great agony, suffering untold tortures and staining the grass with their life's blood, lay five young boys, while about 100 feet away, lying near the water's edge, the shattered remains of what was once a steamboat told the awful tale of what had occurred.
>
> Soon, hundreds of people flocked to the scene, and the spectacle was of such a nature that it will live forever in their memories. Bruised, burned and mangled, dripping with blood, with distorted and unrecognizable features, the injured boys, in their terrible pain and distress, called loudly to their loved ones to come to their assistance and alleviate their awful sufferings.

One of the first women on the scene was Mrs. Fetzer, whose children had left home to go fishing that morning. "Where are my boys?" she cried, elbowing her way through the shell-shocked crowd. There are no words in any language ever spoken by the human tongue that could describe how the worried mother must have felt when she reached the wharf and recognized the horribly mutilated body of her 14-year-old son Allen lying cold in death, and her youngest son, Arthur, bloodied and broken, barely clinging to life. Arthur was rushed to Mary Packer Hospital but died hours later.

Roy McDonald, one of the boys who had survived the explosion with minor injuries, gave the following description what had happened:

"I heard a loud noise, and when I turned to look to see what was wrong, I saw a boy which proved to be Allen Fetzer going up in the air. He went as high as the trees along the bank and fell in a pile of wood. Pieces of wood and iron fell in all directions, and I saw several other boys fall in the water, but it came so sudden that I didn't know what happened until the men came."

The men Roy was referring to were Frank Lawrence and Samuel Welker, workmen who were closest to the wharf when the explosion took place. Lawrence stated:

"By the time we reached the ground, an awful sight was ready for our view. The entire roof and side walls of the Montour had been blown to atoms, and ruin was to be seen on every side. The contents of the boat were scattered among the pile of debris, and the machinery on a nearby digger was twisted into an almost useless mass of scrap iron... We got Frank Keller out from under the engine on the coal digger, and the other boys were taken from the water. The body of Allen Fetzer lay along the bank about 25 feet away. We heard him groan once, but before we got to his side, he was dead."

Charles Keller died at the hospital the following night. The twelve-year-old boy had been so severely injured that most people were amazed that he clung to life as long as he did. He had sustained several broken ribs, a severed artery in his shoulder, and was badly burned all over his entire body.

It took two days to locate the pilot of the steamboat, George Frymeyer, who was blown more than one hundred feet out over the river. Frank Keller, from the Sunbury hospital, told investigators that Frymeyer had just put water into the boiler and was standing with his hand on the valve when the boiler exploded.

A party of more than fifty searchers and divers dragged and dredged the river with hooker poles and grappling irons all day Saturday, without success. Two of Frymeyer's brothers were in the search party, going about their ghastly task in stoic silence, never stopping for a moment—not even as their elderly gray-haired father wept from the riverbank.

Fate had been unreasonably cruel to old Mr. Frymeyer. Twenty years earlier, another one of his sons had met his death through the explosion of a boiler at a sawmill in Shamokin Dam.

The remains of the steamboat pilot weren't found until Sunday afternoon. When his corpse was recovered from beneath twenty feet of water, it was evident that he had received the full force of the blast; his entire chest had been caved in, his skull was fractured, and his right leg was dangling by a thread.

On Friday, July 19, the coroner's jury reported that they were unable to find the cause of the explosion and, therefore, nobody could be held responsible for the tragedy. Numerous experts had inspected the wreckage, and, by all accounts, there was no earthly explanation for why the boiler had malfunctioned.

22.

THE STRANGE DEATH OF DAVID MOSKOWITZ

On March 31, 1953, the body of a young newspaper photographer named David Moskowitz was discovered inside the bedroom of his Sunbury apartment. He was found with his hands and feet tied behind his back and dressed in women's clothes. A bottle of chloroform was found near the body. Whether his demise was the result of an incomprehensible murder or an impossibly bizarre suicide, the death of 22-year-old David Moskowitz remains one of Northumberland County's strangest mysteries.

"The body of our murdered son was found in his home at 1045 Susquehanna Avenue, Sunbury, on the evening of March 31, 1953. Someone must have seen the murderers enter or leave the house. If you have a conscience and believe in God, please come forth and let the proper authorities or ourselves know what you saw."

This was the desperate plea of Mr. and Mrs. Abraham Moskowitz, who were in New York City when the sudden, unexpected death of their son occurred. Obviously, the grieving parents would not entertain the possibility that David had taken his own life, but their remark about "murderers" indicates they believed more than one person was responsible. And yet, after a six-year investigation by multiple law enforcement agencies, not a single arrest was ever made in the case.

THE FINDING OF THE BODY

It was Tuesday evening when Clifford Yohn received a phone call from Mr. and Mrs. Moskowitz. Yohn, who was 27 at the time, lived in a second-floor apartment above David, and the young photographer's parents, who were in New York celebrating Passover, became worried when they had not heard from their son. Abraham Moskowitz, who worked as a guard at the federal penitentiary in Lewisburg, telephoned Yohn, asking him to go downstairs to check on David. It was Clifford Yohn who discovered the body, sprawled across the bed. He immediately called the police.

Officers Richard Wheeler and Warren Thoma of the State Police barracks in Shamokin were assigned to the case, along with the Sunbury city police officers H.C. Gass, James Inkrote, and William Hassinger. They stated that David had been bound in women's stockings with a gag in his mouth. They found no signs of a struggle and no signs of burglary or forced entry.

Was it possible that David had adorned himself in women's clothing and tied nylon stockings around his own hands and feet in some sort of perverse self-pleasure session? Was it possible that he had soaked a rag with chloroform before binding himself, and then intentionally lowered his face onto the doused cloth?

Surely this would explain why there had been no signs of a struggle or forced entry, though it is difficult to imagine why anyone would attempt such a bizarre stunt. Considering the known facts and circumstances, the coroner was convinced that David's death had been a murder, plain and simple.

On April 1, Northumberland County coroner Sidney Kallaway declared that Moskowitz "definitely was the victim of a homicide." Meanwhile, an autopsy was being performed at the Dornsife Funeral Home. The autopsy showed that the young man had died from asphyxiation. Mrs. Moskowitz identified the clothes her son had been wearing as her own.

Since the victim's father was a guard at a federal prison, the logical explanation was that David's murder had been motivated by revenge. From mobsters Whitey Bulger, John Gotti, and Henry Hill (whose life inspired the hit film *Goodfellas*) to labor boss Jimmy Hoffa and Soviet spy Alger Hiss, the Lewisburg Federal Penitentiary was home to some of America's most prolific criminals. It was easy to imagine a disgruntled mafia boss ordering a hit on Abraham's son to teach the prison guard a lesson.

But, then again, it was also possible that law enforcement in conservative, rural Pennsylvania had never heard about autoerotic asphyxiation, much less dealt with a case involving it.

The practice of autoerotic asphyxiation has been documented since the 17th century when witnesses at public hangings noticed that male victims often developed an erection, which sometimes resulted in ejaculation. When the carotid arteries on the side of the neck are compressed, the sudden loss of oxygen to the brain induces a semi-hallucinogenic state known as hypoxia. This, in turn, often produces feelings of pleasure. The intensity of the pleasure is further increased when orgasms are brought into the equation.

Of course, accidental death occasionally occurs.

There are numerous famous examples of autoerotic fatalities; INXS frontman Michael Hutchence died from autoerotic asphyxiation in 1997, and actor David Carradine similarly met his death in 2009. British politician Stephen Milligan's death in 1994 was also ruled a case of autoerotic asphyxiation. Although the practice goes back centuries, it was virtually unknown until the 1990s, when *Hustler Magazine* began publishing articles about it. While strangulation is the most common method used to induce hypoxia, various chemicals—such as chloroform—have also been used.

So, what are the odds that a small-town newspaper photographer and part-time grocery store clerk from central Pennsylvania knew about autoerotic asphyxiation and pleasure-inducing effects of chloroform back in 1953?

CURIOSITY AND CHLOROFORM

Police believed that the answer to the riddle of Moskowitz's perplexing death could be obtained from the empty bottle of chloroform found next to the body. Officers conducted a systematic check of all drug stores in the vicinity. They discovered that the only recent purchase of chloroform had been made in October of 1952 by a woman from Sunbury. Police checked with the woman, only to find that the bottle she had purchased was still in her possession.

Stumped by the lack of clues, the authorities called in George Fink, a veteran State Police detective from Harrisburg. Meanwhile, in keeping with the Jewish custom of burying the dead within twenty-four hours, David Moskowitz was laid to rest at the Jewish Cemetery in Northumberland.

The following week started with a startling announcement. On Monday, April 6, Coroner Kallaway announced that no trace of chloroform was found in Moskowitz's body. Because the autopsy indicated that death had taken place about 48 hours before the body was discovered by Clifford Yohn, the coroner theorized that the chloroform could have "dissipated" from the corpse.

But that didn't explain the gag that was in David's mouth, which also showed no traces of chloroform.

State Trooper Richard Wheeler was able to offer a glimpse of hope, however. He told reporters that David Moskowitz had been seen before his death riding in a black car. Authorities were trying their hardest to track down the driver. Unfortunately, they were never able to do so.

A MOTHER TURNS BITTER

Weeks stretched into months, spring gave way to summer, and police had exhausted all possible leads. And as the days shortened and fall turned to winter, David's parents had become so frustrated that they issued a rambling, bitter statement to the public which appeared in the local newspaper. The appeal, entitled "A New Year's Message to the Murderers of Our Son, David" reads:

"You will go out to enjoy what you think will be a happy new year for you, but as there is a God and if you have a conscience, your so-called enjoyment will be but a bitter weight upon your so-called heart.

"Our son, who never harmed anyone but always tried to do good for his fellow man, will lie in his grave, and his soul will be in Heaven looking down upon your rotten, depraved bodies as you go on your rounds of so-called pleasures.

"Do you think that people will keep your secret forever? Don't you know that their consciences will make them reveal who they are? Can people in the know carry such a load on their minds forever? We want to extend our wishes for as happy a new year as we will have, to the murderers and those who know who committed the crime of murdering our son.

"Let us all join in prayers to God in the churches and temples of our different faiths that the perpetrators of this heinous crime be brought to justice. Let us not forget the law of an eye for an eye, a tooth for a tooth, and a life for a life."

Despite the lack of evidence, Mr. and Mrs. Moskowitz insisted that David had been murdered in cold blood and implored the police to continue their investigation. In a last-ditch effort to find a clue, or perhaps to appease Mrs. Moskowitz, State Police Lieutenant Foreman Ramer administered a lie detector test in January of 1955 to an unidentified "person of interest." Although reports do not provide the name of this alleged suspect, contemporary descriptions indicate that it was, likely, Clifford Yohn. Whoever this suspect might have been, the test showed that the person who took the test was innocent.

Based upon the years of fruitless investigation and the lack of clues, motives, and suspects, it seems that the person who most likely killed David Moskowitz was none other than David Moskowitz, who succumbed to his perversions in a manner that would have been unthinkable to the straight-laced residents of the Susquehanna Valley at the time.

23.

THE HUNT FOR HOPSON'S DIAMONDS

(VENANGO COUNTY)

O ne of the greatest treasure hunts in state history took place in October of 1928 after the daredevil airmail pilot "Wild Bill" Hopson suffered a fatal crash near the tiny village of Polk in Venango County. Hopson had been transporting more than $50,000 worth of diamonds (a treasure worth nearly $720,000 in today's currency). Although more than 300 diamonds were eventually recovered, it is believed that nearly one hundred of the valuable gemstones are still out there waiting to be found.

On Thursday, October 18, 1928, the luck of veteran aviator William C. Hopson finally ran out. Hopson, known to friends as "Wild Bill," had been a night flyer for eight years, delivering mail between New York and Cleveland. He had flown the famously dangerous Bellefonte-Cleveland route over the Allegheny Mountains countless times without incident, though many of his colleagues had not been so lucky. This stretch, known as "The Aviator's Graveyard," was riddled with mountain ridges that seemed to be ceaselessly shrouded in fog, making the flight exceedingly dangerous even in the best daytime weather conditions. Because the route crossed over some of the most rugged and sparsely populated terrain in Pennsylvania, even pilots who had been able to survive a crash often succumbed to their injuries long before help arrived.

And so, when a shipment of 900 pounds of mail and a fortune in jewels had to be delivered to Cleveland in the dead of night, Hopson was chosen for the mission, and he accepted the assignment with enthusiasm.

Wild Bill, however, failed to reach his destination.

Shortly before 7 o'clock on the morning of October 18, Hopson's body, charred and mangled beyond recognition, was located by Polk residents J.C. Hays, Ross Perry, and Russ McKissick. The pilot was discovered inside the wreckage of his plane, on a rocky slope overlooking Bear Hollow, approximately three miles south of Polk.

It was Ross Perry who had heard the plane the night before. Although he was not an aviation expert, it was painfully evident from the sound of its engine that something wasn't right. He looked up to the sky and saw the emergency flare that Hopson had dropped but wasn't quite sure what to make of the strange sight, so he went to bed. However, in the morning, he happened to catch a radio report on WLBW about the missing plane, and so he rounded up his friends and ventured to the spot where he had seen the flare.

It was a sickening sight that greeted the three men; the aircraft was broken in two, with much of the twisted, blackened, still-smoldering wreckage clinging to the coniferous trees like gruesome Christmas ornaments. The plane's engine was embedded deep into the rocky soil, while struts and other chunks of the aircraft were strewn across the ground, along with the plane's cargo. It was evident that Hopson's plane had smashed into the hillside nose first; unable to take evasive action, Wild Bill was killed instantly.

Just as the men reached the crash site, they heard search planes approaching. One landed atop Gurney Hill, while another circled overhead. This plane was piloted by Wesley Smith, superintendent of the Bellefonte-Cleveland division, who had joined the search from the Clarion airport. Unbeknownst to Ross Perry and his friends, the fliers weren't just interested in recovering Hopson's body, but the valuable treasure he had been transporting.

On Friday morning, hundreds of residents braved the chill and rugged terrain of Bear Hollow to get to the crash site. Somehow or another, it had been leaked that Hopson was delivering a shipment of jewels from a New York firm, and by afternoon these rumors were confirmed when a woman managed to dig up a handful of small diamonds. News of this discovery spread like wildfire; the October 20, 1928 edition of the *Franklin News-Herald* stated: As a result, the line of cars on the highway at Polk was almost without precedent, while other scores of people sought among the ruins of the burned plane for some trophy of value.

Superintendent Smith, to disperse the gem-crazed mob of treasure seekers, told reporters that the rumors of diamonds were false. But, by this time, the woman who had dug up 14 of the gems was already in Polk trying to sell them, and the hunger for unearned wealth had been so great that it caused one ghoulish fiend to steal the wedding ring from the dead pilot's finger before his remains could be removed from the crash site. It was now apparent to Smith that the federal government needed to step in and restore order.

Postal Inspector William Tafel, of Erie, issued a statement threatening severe fines and criminal charges for anyone who was found to have Hopson's diamonds. By the following Tuesday, more than 300 of the diamonds had been turned over to authorities. The police also made a list of 87 persons who were believed to have the missing diamonds, and these individuals were given 24 hours to turn over the stones. Many of the treasure hunters complied, handing over not just their diamonds, but also Federal Reserve notes, negotiable securities and other loot they had plundered from the crash site. However, subsequent reports indicate that only three-quarters of the diamonds were ever recovered, which means that several of the precious gems are still out there waiting to be found.

24.

HERMAN SCHULTZ

(PIKE COUNTY)

O nly one man has ever lost his life on the scaffold behind the historic Pike County Courthouse in Milford. In some ways, this is a remarkable fact, considering that the cupola-topped red brick courthouse has stood at the corner of Broad and High streets since 1873. Yet the county's first—and only—execution wouldn't occur until twenty-four years after the last brick had been laid into place.

The whole story of Herman Schultz and his execution is remarkable; he was initially cleared of any wrongdoing in the death of his wife, and he may have lived to a ripe old age had it not been for his two sons, who ultimately sent him to the gallows in December of 1897.

Herman Paul Schultz arrived in this country sometime in the 1870s and took for his wife, a lovely young woman named Lizzie Kiefer. They settled in New York City, sharing the same dream of freedom and prosperity that had lured countless other German immigrants away from their homeland to America's shining shores. While Lizzie raised the couple's three boys, Herman worked his way up the ladder of success, eventually managing a chain of tailoring shops in New York. But, on the home front, Schultz's American dream was rapidly becoming a nightmare; their marriage was marred by frequent drunken quarrels and separations. After a suspicious fire destroyed Schultz's tailoring shop on Spring Street, he found work as a bartender.

In July of 1896, Lizzie made up her mind to leave for good. She went to Shohola, taking the children with her, and found employment under the alias of Lydia Smith as a housekeeper at the High Point House, an inn owned by John Wohlfardt. On September 18, 1896, Herman took a trip to Shohola and spent Sunday night at High Point House, where his estranged wife was living. By all accounts, it appeared that the couple had reconciled their differences.

According to Mrs. Wohlfardt, the woman she knew only as "Mrs. Smith" had told her that she was a widow. But after Herman's sudden appearance, she told the mistress of the house that Herman was an old friend who was expecting to inherit a vast fortune from a relative in Germany and that they were going to New York to get married. Mrs. Wohlfardt described the couple as being deeply affectionate toward each other.

At around nine o'clock that evening, Lizzie sent her twelve-year-old son Charles to bed in an adjoining room, and she and Herman stayed up late talking. Around midnight, however, Mrs. Wohlfardt was awakened by a loud bang. Thinking that the cat had knocked over some cooking utensils in the kitchen downstairs, she went back to sleep.

When Lizzie Schultz, alias "Lydia Smith," failed to show up for breakfast on Monday morning, Mrs. Wohlfardt sent another servant, Mrs. Haas, upstairs to fetch her. Mrs. Haas knocked on the door, but there was no answer. As she turned toward the stair, Mrs. Haas heard a man's voice, screaming, "Oh my God! Lizzie is shot!"

Mrs. Wohlfardt raced up the stairs and burst into the room, where she discovered Lizzie's body. There was a bullet hole in her right temple, and Herman's revolver in her hand. When Coroner Geiger arrived at the scene, he scoffed at the notion of suicide; he immediately placed Herman Schultz under arrest.

Some exciting and outlandish revelations were unearthed at the inquest. Charles, the twelve-year-old son, admitted that Herman Schultz was his father and that his parents had been married for nineteen years. Herman had beaten Lizzie numerous times and was a frequent inmate at Blackwell's Island as a result.

Herman, however, fervently insisted that he had slept through the shot that had killed his wife. He also claimed that Lizzie was chronically unfaithful, and even produced an affidavit with her signature admitting this fact. He also produced letters, purportedly written by Lizzie, that he had received during their separation. In these letters, Lizzie begged Herman to come back and promised that she would change her evil, cheating ways.

The coroner's jury, presented with only circumstantial evidence, concluded that Lizzie Schultz came to her death from a gunshot at the hand of some unknown person. Herman was released from jail and beat a hasty retreat to New York, only to find the police waiting for him—his son had turned him in for arson. On Tuesday afternoon, September 22, Lizzie's body was buried in Shohola.

But, if the allegations of abuse presented at the inquest were the work of a young boy's imagination, Charles was just getting warmed up. Herman's twelve-year-old son came out with a sensational accusation against his father, which led to Herman's arrest.

"My father was a tailor," began a statement written by Charles Schultz, "and he opened a store on Spring Street. Sometime later, the place was set on fire, and he collected $500 insurance. After that, on account of trouble with the neighbors, he moved to 14th Street and opened another store. His business prospered so that after a time, he took the whole building and insured his stock for $2,000.

"One night a strange man slept in the store and father, who always allowed the fire to go out at night, saw that it was kept burning on that occasion. Well, we all had to run for our lives, and when I was going out, I saw father dash a jar containing liquid on the floor, which immediately blazed up. He did not get all his insurance, however, so he moved back to Spring Street and, after a time, to 411 West 26th Street."

Charles also claimed that, three years earlier, he saw his brother Willie carrying gallons of benzene and turpentine into the store. He then watched his father and Willie sprinkle the liquid on the floor. Later that night, the building burned to the ground. "My mother's life was insured at the time for $1,000, and I believe part of his plan was to burn her up with the store," he stated. Willie Schultz later confessed to helping his father sprinkle the flammable liquids, though he claimed he had no idea why his father had asked him to do it.

After Schultz had been arraigned and remanded into custody, he told a New York reporter that his arrest had been the result of his son's spite. "He has always been a bad boy," said Herman, "and has given me a heap of trouble up to the present time."

These new allegations from Charles Schultz, along with mounting public pressure, convinced Pike County authorities to take another look at Lizzie's death. He was indicted, tried, and convicted of first-degree murder. On July 20, 1897, he was sentenced to death by hanging.

Shortly after 11 o'clock on the morning of December 7, 1897, Herman Schultz was led to the gallows by Sheriff Courtright. When asked by the executioner if he had any last words, the condemned man read a rather bizarre prepared statement:

"My last wish and desire on this earth is that the skull of my wife, which I believe is in the possession of Dr. Wenner of this town, shall be placed with my dead body in one and the same coffin and shall get buried together."

Schultz's dying wish was never granted, however.

Not only was the hanging of Herman Schultz the first execution in Pike County history, but it also made headlines for being the cheapest hanging in the history of the United States up to that point, costing the county a total of $13, all of which went to the prosecutor.

The additional $15 that had been allocated by county commissioners for the execution was recovered after they sold Schultz's body to the medical school at the University of Pennsylvania for the same amount. They saved money further by "borrowing" a scaffold from adjacent Sullivan County in New York. As for the rope used to hang Schultz, the sheriff paid for that out of his pocket.

25.

THE PUZZLING ORIGINS OF PUZZLETOWN

(BLAIR COUNTY)

S ituated halfway between the city of Altoona and Blue Knob, the second-highest mountain in the state, is a tiny rural village in Blair County's Freedom Township with the curious name of Puzzletown.

Ever since its founding sometime around 1840, people have wondered about the name of this village and several theories have been proposed as to its origin, the most logical being a matter of topography; when viewed on a map, the multitude of public roads and private driveways all seem to converge at a single point at various, odd angles. Puzzletown Road, without warning, suddenly becomes Blue Knob Run Road, though one could easily become confused and find themselves on Noel Lane or Hite Lane instead, while those traveling north on Blue Knob Run Road might accidentally find themselves on Poplar Run Road instead of Puzzletown Road. And then there will those who will pull off onto the shoulder and weep once they realize that Blue Knob Road, Blue Knob Run Road, and Knob Road are not the same thing.

Drivers from out of the area could easily go insane without GPS, as the seemingly random junctions and unexpected forks can take you to all sorts of places with names as strange as Puzzletown. For instance, if you're heading north on Poplar Run Road, you will discover, rather abruptly, that the highway splits just north of Puzzletown, and those who veer right will find themselves on Valley Forge Road heading not toward the famous Valley Forge, but the Duncansville "suburb" of Foot-of-Ten. And, since you're probably wondering, the reason the village is called Foot-of-Ten is that it lies at the foot of the tenth incline plane of the old Allegheny Portage Railroad.

As for Puzzletown, the name has nothing at all to do with confusing roads. It also has nothing to do with crosswords, jigsaws, or riddles. The village is allegedly named in honor of a resident—"Puzzle" Stiffler—of whom very little, if anything, is known.

Puzzletown was initially settled in 1840 by a man named Baird (or Beard, depending on the source), who sold village lots, in the hope of becoming wealthy, and established the Poplar Run post office. Baird never became wealthy as a result of land speculation; the 1883 *History of Huntingdon and Blair Counties* describes Puzzletown, unflatteringly, as, "not a prominent or active place, yet it boasts of one or two small stores, a practitioner of medicine, and a house of worship owned by the United Brethren."

The date when Poplar Run officially became Puzzletown is unclear. However, the earliest mention of Puzzletown in print comes from March of 1877, when the *Cambria Freeman* newspaper mentioned a fire at James McConnel's store: "It puzzles the people of Puzzletown to determine the origin of the fire, whether it was caused by spontaneous combustion or was the work of an incendiary."

THE LEGEND OF OLD PUSSY

Some light was shed on the matter of the origin of the name a few years later in a letter to the editor of the *Harrisburg Telegraph*. The following explanation, as provided by a Duncansville resident referred to only as J.M.G., appeared in the *Telegraph* on August 4, 1879:

"The proper name of the village you refer to is Marion. The post office is called Poplar Run. A post office in Franklin County, Pa., being named Marion, this office could not take the name of the village, and hence named after the stream passing through it—the village, not the office.

"You must permit me to give you a short history of why it is called Puzzletown. The proprietor laid out his town and called it Marion, applied for a license, and opened a hotel. He was a man in body about five feet five or six inches in height and in weight about 180 pounds, and from forty-five to fifty years, and predisposed to corpulency, so that in a few years of playing landlord of the Marion Hotel, and whether from eating or drinking or both, true it was that his heft had increased to three hundred pounds and upwards, his stately step was changed into a rolling waddle—in short, he became a remarkable man (of the sort), and consequently someone (to the historian unknown) named him 'Old Pussy.'

"The plebeians of the neighborhood, being of different nationalities, could or did not stick to the original, which degenerated into Old Pusly, Old Pussely and finally Old Puzly. The old proprietor now died and was gathered to his fathers in the valley of Poplar Run, and his kind neighbors and citizens of the valley, in memory of kindness received, could not suffer his last name to sink into oblivion but applied it to the town.

"But Puzlytown did not sound well, nor look well on paper. Finally, application having been made to the schoolmaster, it was put into good Saxon, to wit—Puzzletown."

The amount of truth or accuracy contained in this strange explanation is unclear, but if "J.M.G." knew what he was talking about, it would imply that Puzzletown wasn't named after a vague, shadowy character named Stiffler, but the founder of the village, known only to history as Baird. There might be a grain of truth in this theory, however; a 1928 article from the *Duncannon Record* about the village's history asserts that, in earlier times, the place in question was known as Pudzletown or "Pussly's Town," in memory of 'Puzzle' Stiffler, who, according to the *Duncannon Record*, was an innkeeper. So perhaps "J.M.G." had confused Baird with Stiffler.

THE GREAT NAME DEBATE OF 1928

At any rate, the reputation of Puzzletown received a boost in the early 1920s due to several construction projects that brought new highways, bridges, and other much-needed infrastructure to the sparsely populated area. It was around this time that some of the locals began expressing a desire to see the village return to its intended name of Marion, in honor of the famous Revolutionary War hero, Gen. Francis "Swamp Fox" Marion.

In 1927 county government took control over the newly paved highway running through the heart of Puzzletown, a move that promised to bring more traffic through the sleepy village. One lifelong resident named Frank Treml, whose father had been the village blacksmith back when the place was known as Poplar Run convinced members of the Blair County Motor Club that the name ought to be changed to Marionsville. The motor club agreed and took it upon themselves to erect "Welcome to Marionsville" signs along the highway. Those who preferred Puzzletown, however, were enraged by this act, and the matter ultimately had to be resolved by the state government.

Of course, opinions in the village were sharply divided; half of the citizens wanted to keep the Puzzletown name, while the other half believed that it was only proper to honor the wishes of the village's founder (even though nobody was one hundred percent sure what that was). Things got so heated that some folks wrote scathing letters to local newspapers, demanding that they stop referring to their hometown as Puzzletown, or Marionsville, depending on what side of the argument they were on.

One such angry letter, written by Mrs. Archie McIntosh, was published by the *Altoona Tribune* on March 26, 1928:

> In writing of the road from Newry to Marionsville you have used Puzzletown. Is the *Tribune* not a wide-awake newspaper? Does it not know that Puzzletown was but a nickname and has recently been wiped off the map and Marionsville reinstated? Marionsville is the original and correct name for this little village. It was named in honor

of the redoubtable General Francis Marion, who helped fight the British in the Revolutionary War. That beautiful poem by Bryant called 'The Song of Marion's Men' was written for this same general who won such great renown in the history of the nation. Can you understand or find fault with us for being both proud and happy on having the name reinstated? We hope the *Altoona Tribune* in the future will give its hearty cooperation by using Marionsville entirely. It is still used in court, in real estate transfers, and it is on the deeds on record of property situated here in the village.

A blistering letter written by a man with an opposing point of view, H. Beam Piper, was later published in the *Altoona Tribune*:

As you quite likely know, the little community of Puzzletown, not far from Blue Knob, has been plunged into turmoil and strife lately because a certain element of the inhabitants are anxious to have the name changed from its present one, so-called after 'Puzzle' Stiffler, noted local character, to Marionsville, in honor of the Revolutionary general who, I do not believe, ever set foot in Pennsylvania, but who already has half a dozen townships, towns, and villages named after him in this state.

This would, of course, be nothing short of a crime, and because of the commotion raised over it, I decided to go down and take a look at it. I thought I had come to one of the battlefields of the World War. On the road leading into town, in the front yard of a farmhouse, I saw a big white sign some eight feet in length, reading: "We Welcome You to Puzzletown"... In the village proper, the other group have their sign, about three by three feet, "Welcome to Marionsville." The Puzzletown machine gunners seem to have taken a most violent exception to this sign, for it looks as if it had been wrenched down, apparently with a crowbar, and is now held up by about half a hundred nails. There are also a great number of holes in it that could only have been made by rifle balls.

Piper's letter must have settled the matter for the *Tribune*; the editor responded by declaring: "'Puzzle' Stiffler's name must be retained at all costs. The 'puzzle' is that people residing in a town which has a unique and colorful name should want to give it a name already in use in various parts of Pennsylvania, thereby causing confusion to residents, post office officials, and travelers. There is only one Puzzletown, and there was only one 'Puzzle' Stiffler, and Blair County is proud that both were products of the county; long may the name prevail, for we shall never see their like again."

This was a remarkable victory for the pro-Puzzletown faction since the paper's editor happened to be the highly esteemed author, folklorist and historian Henry W. Shoemaker, who had publicly argued in the beginning that the name of the village should be Marionsville.

THE STATE SETTLES THE DEBATE

On March 28, 1928, the State Geographic Board ruled in favor of Puzzletown, denying an appeal to the board to have the village officially recognized as Marionsville. Ironically, on the very same day, Mrs. Archie McIntosh vehemently denied having written the pro-Marionsville letter that had been published just two days earlier. My opinion is that she did write that letter, but feared retribution and possible ex-communication by the same pro-Puzzletown neighbors who had shot holes in the "Welcome to Marionsville" sign. Or perhaps Mrs. McIntosh just wanted to be on the right side of history.

But, despite the State Geographic Board's ruling, it took some time for life to get back to normal in the tiny rural village. Shortly after the ruling, the man who had erected the enormous "We Welcome You to Puzzletown" sign, David Yingling, reported that someone had stolen it, posts and all. Several months would pass before the villagers finally came to terms with the board's decision.

Today the controversy is long forgotten, and the name Puzzletown still appears in newspapers and on maps, although the truth behind the origin of the name will long remain a Blair County puzzle.

26.

THE MULESHOE CURVE SUICIDE GRAVE

(BLAIR COUNTY)

The William Penn Highway, which ran from New York City to Pittsburgh, winds through the states of New York, New Jersey, and Pennsylvania and is stitched together from many different highways. Today, this historic auto trail, or at least the portion of it running through Blair County, is better known as Old Route 22. Drivers along this scenic route will be rewarded with breathtaking views. They will pass a unique topographical feature known as "The Muleshoe," a curve-shaped mountain gap in the Allegheny Mountains in the vicinity of Gallitzin Spring.

For several decades, motorists along this stretch also encountered a sight that was less than charming—a crude, shallow grave next to the highway marked with a simple, plain wooden cross.

This would be the grave of a man whose name has never been ascertained, a suicide victim who, in July of 1905, was found hanging from a tree by a liquor dealer named John Becker. Astounded by his discovery, Becker ran to tell the first person he encountered, which happened to be John

Undated postcard of the original PRR culvert at Muleshoe Curve

F. Goldy, proprietor of the nearby Fountain Inn, and the two men then notified the authorities. Goldy, better known as "Cappy" in those parts, was a colorful fellow from Scotland. Since the inn was of some historical significance, it is worth devoting a few paragraphs to the illustrious establishment before we get back to the mystery of the unknown suicide victim.

The Fountain Inn, built during the era of stagecoaches and operated by John Fries until the late 1850s, was one of the most famous lodging places in America at one time. During its heyday, when it was owned by James Maitland, the inn provided shelter to scores of celebrity guests, including President Van Buren, P.T. Barnum, and the "Swedish Nightingale" Jenny Lind. The inn derived its name from the "Font-of-Eight," an equally famous mountain spring a half-mile away, and stood at the site of the present-day Muleshoe Reservoir. According to historical records, dozens of large trout were kept in a pool at the inn, and guests would point to the fish they desired to eat, which would then be caught in a net by the chef and prepared to taste. Sadly, the historic inn was destroyed by fire in 1908.

Shortly afterward, the property was purchased by the Pennsylvania Railroad and torn down to make way for the reservoir. As for Goldy, he was shot in 1908 by an unknown assailant who showed up at his house with a revolver. The man fired at him as soon as Goldy opened the door and then fled into the woods. Although the gunshot wound was not fatal, the affair took a toll on his health, and he passed away in June of 1909 at the age of 65.

A different establishment, the "New Fountain Inn," was built in 1920, about a mile away from where the historic tavern once stood.

BURIAL OF THE SUICIDE VICTIM

After Becker and Goldy had notified the authorities, they returned to where the body was hanging. They discovered the dead man's coat lying nearby and a wallet containing $25.90 but found no clue that could help identify him. Soon the deputy coroner, H.W. McCartney, arrived, accompanied by undertaker C. Liebegott, Mr. Bridenbaugh of the county almshouse, and a handful of curiosity seekers from Duncansville and Gallitzin. They scoured the woods for clues but came up empty-handed. Because the body of the victim, who was hanging from a tree by a belt, was so badly decomposed, it was impossible to tell what his face had looked like in life.

Undertaker Liebegott's two sons, Luther and George, were assigned the task of burying the body, along with Samuel Keller, who was employed as the caretaker of that particular stretch of highway, which was known as the Pittsburgh-Philadelphia Turnpike at the time. The body was buried about 150 yards from where it had been found, just beyond the shoulder of the road.

Although the body was never identified, the clothes matched the description of those that were worn by a man who, two weeks earlier, had checked into the Norman Hotel in Duncansville. The man, who appeared to be around 45 years of age, spoke English well but had a hint of a foreign accent. He had been seen at the hotel asking for directions to Johnstown.

A DEVOTED CARETAKER

Samuel Keller never stopped thinking about the unfortunate man he had buried alongside the highway in July of 1905. For more than three decades, he visited the grave dutifully every Memorial Day. He placed an American flag atop the burial mound, which had since been planted with lilies, irises,

Postcard of Fountain Inn, circa 1898

and other wildflowers and marked with a wooden cross. Every spring and summer, when the flowers would bloom, the decorated burial mound presented a curious and colorful spectacle to passing motorists up until 1929, when the grave was moved to a different location.

In 1929, when that stretch of roadway was relocated to bypass a dangerous curve, the new highway had to pass directly over the grave of the unknown suicide victim. Keller, who was still employed as the highway caretaker at the time, considered it his duty to make sure that the body was properly and respectfully disinterred. Keller, assisted by several members of the highway construction crew, opened the grave and found that the original casket had decayed entirely; all that remained were bones, a scrap of a leather belt, a dime that had been in the dead man's pocket at the time of his burial, and the metal handles of the coffin. All these objects were placed into a small box except for the dime, which Keller kept as a souvenir.

A new grave was dug approximately fifty feet from the south side of the new highway and marked with a white wooden cross. Keller continued to tend the grave for the remainder of his life—a devoted caretaker to the very end—and arranged for his son to take over the job when he passed away.

27.

A SOLDIER'S SKELETON AND A TRAGIC LOVE STORY

(LAWRENCE COUNTY)

In March of 1893, a miner by the name of Martin was sent by a group of land speculators to inspect the abandoned Myra & Culbertson ore mine in Plain Grove Township, Lawrence County, to examine the quality and quantity of remaining ore, which the owners of a local railroad planned to extract. What Mr. Martin found, however, was the solution to a western Pennsylvania mystery dating back to the days of the Civil War.

Martin, working under the direction of the Western New York & Pennsylvania Railroad, was called upon to look for mineral deposits on the railroad's proposed line between Eastbrook and Ellwood City. He was particularly fascinated by the old Myra & Culbertson mine, a few miles west of Slippery Rock. The mine had opened sometime in the 1850s but was abandoned a few decades later when the ore became too difficult and expensive to extract. With new mechanical and technological advances, however, the owners of the railroad believed that it was now possible to work the mine profitably. So Mr. Martin and his son Edward went to have a look.

The mine had been abandoned for so long that when Martin and his son arrived, on the morning of Friday, March 3, the entrance was nearly undetectable. After locating an opening, the men crawled on their hands and knees for about six hundred feet until they reached a large chamber. Martin raised his lantern, and, much to his horror, his light fell upon a human skeleton sitting on a ledge, chained to a post.

"The flesh was dried to the bones, which were intact, and the awful spectacle so overcame me that my first impulse was to run, which I started to do," said Martin to the *Pittsburgh Daily Post*. "But on second thought I stopped, called to my son, who was some distance behind me, and when he came up, we re-entered the chamber together. Beside the skeleton lay the rust-eaten barrel and the crumbling stock of an old gun, evidently an old-time musket.

"When I touched the chain that held the skeleton to the post, the links fell apart, and the ghastly frame toppled over and fell to the floor of the mine. The incident startled us... we wanted to get out into the open air again as soon as possible."

After scrambling out of the mine, the two men went into town to report their discovery, and an old farmer related the sad story of a heartbroken young soldier named John Baird.

In 1861, when Captain Samuel Bentley issued a call for volunteers to fight the Confederacy, John Baird of the tiny Worth Township village of Jacksville was among the first to enlist, leaving his bride of a few months behind to keep the home fires burning. Like many soldiers and supporters of the Union, Baird believed that the fighting would be over in the blink of an eye. But as the weeks stretched into months and the war showed no signs of coming to an end, the young private's spirits began to fall. But he soldiered on, because that is what soldiers do, and before long a year had come and gone. It was a miserable life, the painful monotony of long marches in cheap boots broken only by bloody spasms of ferocious, desperate fighting. Only the letters from his wife made his existence tolerable.

Then, one day, John received a letter from Jacksville, but it was not written by his lover's hand. The letter informed him that his wife was dying of consumption. John obtained a furlough and raced back to Worth Township, but it was too late—he got there just in time only to see her coffin being lowered into the ground.

During his year of military life, John had seen more death than any man ought to be allowed to see in a hundred lifetimes, but nothing he had endured on the field of battle steeled him enough to accept the death of his beloved young wife. Yet he put on a brave face, and after the funeral, he grabbed his musket and left town, telling his friends and neighbors that he was going back to the front.

The war eventually came to an end, but John Baird failed to return home. His friends and relatives made inquiries but were informed by the army that the young private never came back from his furlough. The military authorities, believing that John was a deserter, had done an exhaustive search, but no trace of the missing soldier was ever found.

The locals put all the pieces of the puzzle together, revealing the sad story of John Baird's final days. Baird, overcome with grief, was determined to join his wife on the other side. After chaining himself to a post to ensure that he could not change his mind, he waited for the cold embrace of death, hundreds of feet beneath the earth, in a lonely spot where he knew that his cries for help could not be heard.

While it could not be conclusively proven that the skeleton found by Mr. Martin and his son inside the abandoned Myra & Culbertson mine was that of the lost soldier, the facts seemed convincing enough. On March 6, 1893, the bones were taken from the mine and buried in a grave alongside his wife at the old Jacksville graveyard.

28.

THE ROYALTON ARMY TRANSPORT PLANE CRASH OF 1929

(DAUPHIN COUNTY)

One of the saddest aviation disasters on state record occurred in the Harrisburg suburb of Royalton on the afternoon of January 11, 1929, when a Fokker C-2 cargo plane crashed shortly after taking off from the Middletown Air Depot.

Opened as a supply depot for U.S. Army Signal Corps aircraft in 1917, the Middletown airfield served as an important support installation to the Air Force for several decades. It was reborn as Olmsted Air Force Base in 1948—a name that endured until the base was closed down in 1969.

While several accidents involving military aircraft have taken place near Middletown, the crash of the Fokker C-2 was the deadliest, claiming the lives of eight soldiers and leading the aviation industry to make changes that have undoubtedly saved numerous lives in the years following the tragedy at Royalton.

A FORTUITOUS COIN FLIP

It was shortly after 1:45 on a bitter cold Friday afternoon when Lieutenant Henry Robert Angell assumed command of the plane, which had arrived at Middletown earlier that morning from Bolling Field in Washington, DC, with Captain Harry A. Dinger at the helm, to load up with supplies. Captain Dinger then took off in an amphibian plane for Washington with a sergeant by the name of Mayland, believing that the C-2 was following closely behind. He did not receive word that Lieutenant Angell's aircraft had crashed until he landed at Bolling Field.

One of the strange details of the disaster is that Lt. Angell and Capt. Dinger flipped a coin to decide who would fly the cargo plane back to Washington.

According to witnesses on the ground, the C-2 failed to gain altitude after takeoff, and dove nose-first into the ground, narrowly missing several houses and crashing with a thunderous explosion in a vacant Penn Street lot adjacent to the Royalton post office and the Guy Vogt meat packing plant. A resident, Frank Geisinger, said, "I saw the plane start out, and everything seemed to be going all right when suddenly it seemed to buckle, and then it fell, turning over and over several times."

ANGELL BEGS FOR DEATH

Airfield officials and rescue crews, led by army doctor J.F. Blecker, raced to the scene, but only found confusion among the wreckage and crushed bodies. Although the pilot had managed to survive, five of the passengers were killed instantly. Because the soldiers had come from Bolling Field and were unknown to the men at Middletown, identification proved difficult. "They were strangers to us," said Captain Frederick S. Christine, commander of the Middletown Air Depot. "Just landed here this morning, and we hardly knew any except the officers."

Three of the crewmen, including Lieutenant Angell, were rushed to local hospitals. Angell was transported to Harrisburg Hospital with several broken bones and severe head injuries. Dr. Kunkel, who examined the pilot, found that Angell had broken more bones than he could count.

Here is H. H. Lerch, of 2542 Lexington street, Harrisburg, who was with his parents in Royalton when the Army Fokker transport plane C-2 crashed yesterday with fatal results to right occupants. He helped pull the dead and dying from the wreckage. Other pictures appear on Page 7.

Miraculously, but perhaps cruelly, Lieutenant Angell never lost consciousness. After he had been cut out of the cockpit with an ax and carried to a waiting ambulance, he implored the driver to kill him to extinguish his agony. "Shoot me. For God's sake, shoot me," cried the pilot to Charles Sheaffer, who rode with the mortally wounded airman to the hospital.

"The screams coming from the plane were terrible," recalled Royalton resident Carolyn Holland. "The rescuers who reached the scene just a moment before I had a terrible time getting the passengers out. One man, I think it was the pilot, was in terrible agony... his legs were evidently broken, and one of his feet was almost off. He seemed to want to die."

Angell succumbed to his injuries within the hour, however, and his co-pilot, Mike Kelly, would die of his injuries two minutes later. By four o'clock that afternoon, only one of the men who had climbed aboard the cargo plane would still be among the living; Sergeant Patrick Conroy, a native of New York City. As the only surviving witness, aviation officials hoped that Conroy could tell what had gone wrong, but that spark of hope was extinguished when Conroy arrived at the hospital without a pulse. It was soon evident that he would never recover.

That the cargo plane should crash at all mystified officials; mechanics had given the plane a clean bill of health immediately before takeoff, and when it came to the Fokker C-2, the mechanics at Middletown knew the aircraft better than anyone. Just days earlier, a modified Army Air Corps Fokker C-2A intriguingly named "?" (referred to only as "Question Mark") shattered world records in several different categories during a 150-hour nonstop flight. It was the aviation mechanics at Middletown Air Depot who had outfitted the plane, allowing it to make numerous successful in-flight refuelings during its record-setting six days in the air.

This is just another strange detail surrounding the Royalton tragedy; the same mechanics who worked on the C-2A that stayed aloft for 150 straight hours from January 1-6 also worked on the C-2 that could not stay aloft for more than 60 seconds on January 11, even though the planes were virtually identical.

RACING THE REAPER

The five crewmen who died at the scene were identified as Master Sergeant Joseph B. McCarthy and Staff Sergeant Rudolph Lehutta, both of Washington, DC, Staff Sergeant Henry Cronan of Tacoma Park, Maryland, Private Samuel B. Jones of Bellbuckle, Tennessee, and Private Clarence Birch of Chicago. Lieutenant Angell, a native of Birmingham, Alabama, died shortly after he arrived at the hospital, as did co-pilot Mike Kelly. Five of the eight victims are buried at Arlington National Cemetery. Kelly is buried in Frackville, Schuylkill County.

Meanwhile, in a hospital room in Washington, a 24-year-old army nurse struggled frantically to pull herself out of bed. Charlotte Bucker, bedridden for five days with tonsillitis, had just gotten word that her fiance, Patrick Conroy, was clinging to life at a hospital in Harrisburg. Despite her weakened condition, she returned home and rummaged through her closet until she found her prettiest hat and the blue dress that her fiance loved so much. She knew that Pat would never regain consciousness, but she wanted to look nice for him, just in case the Lord decided to deliver a miracle. She then raced to the railroad station and caught the first train to Harrisburg.

Sadly, her efforts were in vain; Patrick Conroy died ten minutes before she arrived. Their wedding had been planned for the following month. Charlotte, overcome with grief, collapsed. She returned to Washington the following day, the few hours she had spent as a stranger in a strange city would be etched into her memory until the day of her death in 1960, at the age of 55. She never married.

A GRUESOME RECORD AND A LASTING LEGACY

At the time of the crash, the tragedy at Royalton entered the history books as the deadliest aviation disaster in American history up to that point, surpassing the crash of a Ford tri-motor transport aircraft in Texas that claimed five lives the preceding year. This was still the era of single and double-seated airplanes, and transport planes were a recent invention. As a result, the tragedy was covered by newspapers around the world, which allowed numerous aviation experts to weigh in on the matter.

The prevailing theory as to what caused the crash was that the cargo inside the plane's fuselage had shifted during takeoff. When Angell attempted to correct, the cargo shifted once again—this time in the opposite direction—causing 15,000 pounds of cargo to pile up on top of the crew. Although it has never been proven, it is possible that some of the men sustained fatal injuries before the Fokker C-2 even crashed into the earth. The official U.S. Army report, however, claims that the plane's left outboard engine failed (mechanics at Middletown strongly disputed this claim). At any rate, losing one of the three engines probably would have caused the cargo to shift anyway, and the statements made by numerous witnesses stating that the plane suddenly took a nosedive seem to support the shifting cargo theory.

While it may seem like common sense today, the cargo carried by transport planes in 1929 was not secured or strapped down; neither was the cargo weighed before being loaded onto the plane. Since transporting cargo by air was uncharted territory, nobody ever thought of considering

—By Staff Photographer.
The only virtually undamaged section of the big tri-motored monoplane transport of the Army Air Corps, wrecked at Middletown yesterday, was the rear of the fuselage and the rudder and tail section, shown in the accompanying photograph. The horizontal red and white stripes of the rudder stand out plainly in the foreground, while the untouched tail surfaces can be seen flanking it.

these things. Other experts speculated that the C-2's three 220-horsepower engines were just not powerful enough for the job.

The crash at Royalton ultimately led to improvements that have undoubtedly prevented similar aviation disasters. The Fokker flown by Lieutenant Angell was one of eleven built for the U.S. Army Air Corps (three C-2 transport planes were built in 1926, and eight C-2A planes were built in 1928. The only difference between the two variants is that the C-2A had a slightly greater wingspan). After the crash, Fokker recalled the C-2As it had built in 1928 and replaced the 220-hp Wright J-5 radial piston engines with Wright J-6-9 radial piston engines, which supplied 330-hp each. These modified cargo planes were re-designated C-7. By 1931, all new production models were fitted with 300-hp engines and redesigned with larger wings and vertical fins.

29.

THE BRUTAL MURDER OF MARY QUINN

(LACKAWANNA COUNTY)

The blood-chilling murder of a young Scranton woman named Mary Quinn remained unsolved for twelve years until an epidemic of rape and physical attacks on young women in nearby Wilkes-Barre finally led police to her killer. This is the tragic tale of the crime; it is a story of unimaginable violence, heartbreak, and the relentless pursuit of justice. And considering that Quinn's slayer received a surprisingly lenient sentence—and went on to rape again after his release from prison—it is also a tale of imperfect justice.

Mary Quinn was a silent, unassuming young woman who was well-liked throughout the neighborhood where she lived, in what is now part of West Scranton. At the turn of the century, this sparsely populated region was known as Keyser Valley, and the Quinn family—comprised of Mary, her sister, and a brother—lived in a mining "company house" on the edge of a field known as Continental Commons.

On the night of June 2, 1902, Mary was alone in the house, baking bread when she realized that she was out of yeast. With the stars to light her path, she decided to cross a field and procure some yeast from a neighborhood store. It was a little after 9 o'clock when she left her house and walked down the lane, stopping to talk with several friends and neighbors along the way. Near the Hyde Park mine shaft, she visited the home of a friend, Mary Herrick, but by the time she had left her friend's house, it was after 10 o'clock, and she realized that it was too late to continue her journey for yeast. She started for home, encountering two policemen near the railroad crossing who warned her that it was not safe for a girl to go unprotected in that part of the valley late at night.

Mary told the officers that she would be fine. After all, she had been born and raised in the vicinity, and she knew every man, woman, and child in the neighborhood. As far as she knew, she didn't have an enemy in the world, and certainly none in Keyser Valley. The policemen sighed, and Mary Quinn continued her journey home, choosing to take the policemen's advice to stick to the main road instead of cutting across Continental Commons, as the field was known in those days. This fateful decision was one that would cost her life.

Not far down the road, she was attacked by a dark figure that leaped from out of the shadows. Mary never had a chance to scream for help; the assailant struck her in the back of the head with a wooden club without warning. With a pool of blood forming on the road around her limp body, the attacker ripped off her clothing. He wasn't sure if the girl was alive or dead, but it made no difference—he raped her anyway, stopping only to drag her body off the road and into a field when he thought he heard someone approaching.

Daylight revealed the attacker's depravity and illuminated the unthinkable brutality of the crime. A trail of blood extended from the spot on the road where she had fallen, over a wooden fence, and into the pasture where her body was found later that evening. Mary's hair comb was found in the road and a clump of her hair on the fence. Investigators surmised that she had regained consciousness at some point; for some horrible reason, the attacker returned to the road where he had dropped his club and came back to the girl and bashed in her forehead, crushing the skull to shards just above the left eye.

The force of the blow was so severe that the girl's skull was crushed into a pulp, and not a whole bone remained... the brain matter was exposed. This silenced her for all time, and the murderer left her for dead and made good his escape. —Philadelphia Inquirer, June 15, 1902.

Before making his escape, the attacker threw his weapon into the bushes, where it was found the following day, covered in blood and hair. Mary's empty yeast bottle, which she had been carrying with her at the time of the brutal assault, was located nearby.

Astonishingly, Mary was still clinging to life when her body was dis-covered shortly before midnight by John Lukas and Joseph Frudowsky, two men who were returning home after their shift in the mines. They had heard a strange moaning sound coming from Continental Commons and went to investigate. When they discovered the bloody body, they ran as fast as they could to the first house they saw—which happened to be the home of the Quinns. It was Mary's brother, John, who opened the door.

"We've found a woman who is half murdered!" gasped Lukas. John summoned a few neighbors—Thomas Sweitzer, Patrick Scott, and Frank Moran—and the party raced to the spot where the body lay. It was Quinn who lit the match and held it to the woman's face. He collapsed when he discovered that he was staring into the face of his sister. The other men called for a doctor, J.J. Brennan, who raced to the scene, but Brennan declared that nothing in the world could be done for the dying girl. They put her body on a makeshift stretcher and carried her to the Quinn house. If nothing else, at least Mary would be able to pass away in her own home, surrounded by those who loved her.

OUTRAGE IN THE ELECTRIC CITY

The rape and murder of Mary Quinn outraged the entire city, and every member of the police force put aside other pursuits to focus on catch-ing the cowardly killer. Meanwhile, the county commissioners put up a substantial reward for information leading to the arrest of the perpetrator. They released the following notice:

"Notice is hereby given that the county of Lackawanna will pay the sum of five hundred dollars reward to the person or persons securing the arrest and conviction of the party or parties responsible for the death of Mary Quinn, who was supposed to have been murdered on the night of the 2d of June, 1902, in Keyser Valley, Scranton, Pa. Signed, John J. Durkin, John Penman, J. Courier Morris, commissioners; E.A. Jones, County Controller."

Police eventually focused their efforts on one individual, a black man by the name of William Perry. He had a criminal history of molesting young women after knocking them unconscious with a wooden wagon tongue wrapped in fabric from a pair of stockings. Although the modus operandi was similar, Perry had a rock-solid alibi and was never charged in connection to Mary Quinn's death.

Just one month after Mary's death, her brother John died at the age of thirty after a long illness attributed to mental deterioration brought on by the death of her sister. His was the fourth death to ravage the Quinn family that year. The mother passed away first, followed by John's twin brother, and then Mary. Only a sister, Anna, remained.

A KILLER'S CONFESSION

The year is now 1914, and the Keyser Valley of Mary Quinn's youth is hardly recognizable. The booming coal business has ushered in waves of new arrivals to Lackawanna County, and the fields of Keyser Valley have all but disappeared, replaced by rows and rows of coal company housing. Census records show that the population of Lackawanna County nearly doubled between the time that Mary Quinn was born to the time of the first breakthrough in the case in 1914.

To put this period into perspective, two weeks after Mary was killed, a rowdy and incorrigible seven-year-old boy named George was enrolled at St. Mary's Industrial School for Boys in Baltimore. Nineteen days before Mary Quinn's killer was finally identified, that same boy was making his first appearance as a professional baseball pitcher for the minor-league Baltimore Orioles. That boy, of course, was George Herman "Babe" Ruth.

In March of 1914, several young girls were molested in Wilkes-Barre in the vicinity of Grove Street. Descriptions of the attacker given by victims led to the arrest of William Pegram, described by newspapers as a "colored degenerate" with a "failing for white women." The 42-year-old Pegram, who was picked up by Sergeant Adam Hergert on March 26 in connection with an attack on a 13-year-old girl from Farley Lane, surprised authorities by confessing to the 1902 murder of Mary Quinn. The admission was so stunning that Chief of Police John Roberts warned Pegram against making statements about the deceased girl, as those statements could be used against him.

Pegram, however, either failed to grasp the seriousness of what he was about to do or simply did not care. He spoke freely about the murder and was subsequently asked by Chief Roberts to write a full confession, which he did. Pegram wrote:

> I was living in Raymond's Court, Scranton, with my sister (Ida Pegram), who kept house for a man named Andrews. I got acquainted with Miss Mary Quinn. I first met her in Hyde Park near the greenhouses. I went to Hyde Park often and other places around the city of Scranton looking for women. During the month I lived there, I did not work. Other times I worked at the Vulcan Iron Works in Wilkes-Barre and went up to Scranton often.
>
> I chased a woman in West Scranton one night. I met her at the turnoff by the greenhouses near a cemetery. I went to have some fun, to fool with her. I met her outside. I went to the prop yard of a mine near her house and got a cart hook or some other club. I hit her in a field, and when she fell down, I dragged her away behind the bushes. Then I went down the steam railroad track to Cannon Ball Depot. I kept out of the way as I did not know whether anybody was watching me or not.

Pegram claimed that in the years following the murder, he kept a low profile by living on the farm of Cabel Ide in Idetown. Some county officials, however, investigated Pegram's story and uncovered several discrepancies. A few believed that he had confessed to the crime merely for notoriety; others suspected that he was mentally imbalanced. "He is a nut," declared Captain Palmer with certainty.

On March 29, after spending three days in the city jail, Pegram was taken to the scene of the crime by City Detectives Connery and Deiter, Captain Palmer, and County Detectives Mitchell and Matthews. They wanted to gauge Pegram's reaction and determine whether he had fabricated his confession. According to the Scranton Republican, the party was besieged by two women, who shouted, "Look at the detectives holding that n----r! He ought to be lynched!" Their cries attracted others until a crowd of over five hundred surrounded the detectives and the accused killer.

"Lynch him! Lynch him!" they chanted in unison until it appeared that Pegram was about to be strung up from the nearest tree. Pegram clutched the arm of Detective Matthews. "Don't let them kill me!" he begged.

Realizing they had to act quickly, the detectives linked arms and formed a circle, with Pegram in the center. They forged through the mob, fending off rocks, bottles, and insults hurled by the angry crowd until they reached Luzerne Street.

The excursion to Continental Commons was an exercise in futility, and when it was over, no one could agree on whether Pegram was telling the truth. "He is a low degenerate," stated Detective Connery to the press, "and his statements cannot be relied upon."

District Attorney George W. Maxey, however, begged to differ, pointing out that Pegram had accurately described the murder weapon and the injuries to Mary Quinn. Even if Pegram had read about these details in published reports, it had been over a decade since Mary's name appeared in print. Maxey claimed that all the discrepancies in Pegram's story pertained to time and place names and chalked up these discrepancies to Pegram's low intelligence. "He simply has his mental wires crossed, that's all," said Maxey.

Pegram was charged with murder, and his trial began on October 19, 1914, before Judge H.M. Edwards. Pegram was defended by court-appointed attorneys Harry W. Mumford and Michael J. Rafter. Mumford, interestingly, refused to argue against his client's sanity. "The negro is not crazy," he told the jury, "but he has the mind of a fourteen-year-old child. Therefore, he is not wholly responsible for his actions."

The jury couldn't decide; they held out for nine days before finally reaching a verdict. Some of the jurors even wrote a letter to Judge Edwards, begging him to put an end to the madness and let them return home. Meanwhile, indignation was running high in the press; it was pointed out that the cost of boarding and feeding the jurors had eclipsed $943, which was a rather exorbitant sum in 1914.

A VERDICT AT LAST

On October 31, the jurors finally returned a verdict. They found William Pegram guilty of second-degree murder and made a recommendation of "extreme mercy" for the killer. This recommendation was probably because two of the holdout jurors were church pastors who had been standing their ground for acquittal. Matters were further complicated when defense attorney Mumford filed a petition for a new trial, claiming that Pegram had been the victim of an unfair and impartial jury. The jury foreman, Rev. Thomas Payne, who happened to be a Universalist minister, was the square peg who had caused the record-setting deadlock, which was the longest in county history.

Judge Edwards scoffed at Mumford's allegation and denied his request for a new trial. He did, however, bow to Payne's recommendation for leniency. And so, even though Pegram had not only confessed to murdering Mary Quinn but to sexually assaulting dozens of women and children as well, he was sentenced to five-to-twenty years in prison (he ended up serving eleven). One Scranton newspaper reported that Sheriff Ben Phillips didn't even bother handcuffing Pegram during the long journey from Scranton to the Eastern Penitentiary in Philadelphia, so strong was the county's desire to show "mercy" to the convicted killer.

The story of the brutal rape and murder of Mary Quinn should serve as a cautionary tale about mercy and leniency. Incarceration did not reform Pegram or permanently alter his habits; in 1925, almost immediately after his release from Eastern State Penitentiary, he was arrested again—this time for raping an eight-year-old boy in Wilkes-Barre. He pleaded guilty to the charge and received a three-year sentence and a $50 fine. After serving that sentence, Judge Jones decided to tack on the remainder of the original sentence for second-degree murder. Pegram was finally paroled again in 1940, leaving prison at the age of 69.

It is unclear when or where William Pegram died, and his last years have been lost to history. However, when his sister Ida passed away in 1951, it was reported that William was still living.

30.

WHO HANGED THE NIGHT WATCHMAN?

(MONTGOMERY COUNTY)

One of Montgomery County's most perplexing mysteries is the 1932 death of Samuel Forti, whose battered body was found hanging in the washroom of the Werner Foundry in Lansdale, where he worked as a night watchman. At various times, authorities believed that Forti's death was the result of suicide, an attack by a burglar, revenge by a jealous lover, and—perhaps strangest of all—the grisly doings a shadowy religious cult.

It was February 18 of 1932 when Forti, a 45-year-old father of ten, was found hanging from improvised gallows in the foundry washroom. He had been bound hand and foot, suspended from a plank sitting across two lockers. Strips of rags, cut from the lining of a man's coat, were used to tie his hands behind his back, while a leather belt had been used to bind the feet. Based upon the victim's injuries, it appeared that Forti had been struck viciously and repeatedly about the face and body while he gasped in the throes of strangulation.

After making his preliminary investigation, Chief of Police Samuel Woffindin proposed a most unusual theory—that Samuel Forti was a member of a secret religious cult and had been murdered because he wished to resign from its ranks.

According to Woffindin, the dead watchman, along with five other men and one woman, belonged to a secret cult that held services every Sunday morning and twice during the week. Woffindin believed that Forti wanted to leave the cult and that the remaining members, fearing exposure, had slain Forti to protect their own identities. Woffindin based his opinion primarily on the fact that a Bible, written in Italian, was missing from Forti's locker. He believed that the inner secrets of the cult were contained in the missing book.

Josephine Forti, the dead man's widow, indicated that she knew about her husband's involvement with the secret religious order, but didn't know much about the cult itself. As far as she knew, Samuel had no known enemies.

Harry Long, the foreman of the foundry, told police that Forti had appeared highly agitated in the days leading up to his death; he was afraid to set foot outside after dark and spent his breaks inside the foundry locker room. It was there, while Forti was eating a sandwich, that he had been struck over the head with a blunt instrument, trussed up, and suspended from the makeshift gallows. Long stated that nothing appeared to have been disturbed or stolen, which seemed to eliminate the possibility that the night watchman had been killed by a burglar. It was Long who had discovered the body shortly after 7:00 A.M. Coroner Ronald H. Dettre of Norristown was summoned to the scene, and an autopsy performed by Dr. John Simpson showed that the watchman's death had been caused by strangulation.

Others, however, clung to the theory that Forti had been killed during a botched robbery attempt.

William Herman, a foundry employee, stated that someone had attempted to enter the foundry three times during the previous week. Forti had thwarted the break-in attempts each time, but on the night of his death, all the foundry windows were unlocked. Herman, who had witnessed one of the break-in attempts, told police that the man who tried to gain entry was "tall, thin and middle-aged."

This unknown man, claimed Herman, came to the foundry three times in one night. During the first attempt, the man had told Forti that his wife was sick and that he needed to use the telephone to call a doctor. After being turned away, the man returned a short while later and tried to convince Forti that his wife was sick. Once again, Forti barred the stranger from entering. Later that same night, Forti reported seeing a man in "high topped shoes" prowling around the grounds with a flashlight.

Supervisors investigated the matter, and it was determined that the incident was caused by Forti's recently developed habit of locking himself inside the washroom. Apparently, the other foundry employees were tired of having to ask the night watchman to unlock the door every time they wanted to use the washroom. While it may have seemed odd at the time that Forti had taken to holing himself up inside the washroom, no one had suspected that Forti might have been trying to hide from something or someone.

Meanwhile, Chief of Police Woffindin continued to explore his unusual theory that Forti had been slain by a religious cult. The detective had learned that the Bible was Forti's most prized possession—he took it to work every day--and the fact that it was the only item in the entire foundry that was missing suggested that it may be a key piece of evidence. However, the missing Bible was eventually located by police inside the Forti home.

But if the Bible had been stolen from Forti's work locker, how did it find its way back to his house?

Woffindin also interviewed three of the suspected cult members. They confirmed the rumor that Forti wanted out of the secret society, which had been formed in Lansdale about seven years earlier. As to the practices and beliefs of the cult, none of the members could use medicine or visit doctors, and healing by faith was one of the order's principle beliefs. They claimed that while their sect was strict, their beliefs and practices were no stranger than those practiced by other religious orders. They certainly did not condone murder, they insisted, nor did they partake in any bizarre occult rituals.

Woffindin told reporters that arrests would soon be made, although he refused to divulge the identities of anyone associated with the religious sect. But it was soon revealed through local gossip that the head of the cult was a woman by the name of Julia Sesantis. Purveyors of local gossip also hinted that Sesantis and Forti, who were both married, were having an affair.

"The suspects have been evasive in their answers, and we are having difficulty getting at the facts," stated Woffindin. "From what they say, I believe this cult is a national organization. It is possible that somebody may have been imported to do this job."

SEARCHING A DEAD MAN'S BIBLE FOR CLUES

Police searched the dead watchman's home on February 20 and located the supposedly stolen leather-bound Bible, which was one of two such books found inside the house. Both were printed in Italian, and an interpreter was brought onto the case. Unfortunately, the books contained few clues, other than the fact that the secret cult went by the name of "Chiesa Christiana Delle Fede Apostalica," or "Church of Christ of Faith in Apostles." It was learned that there was another branch of the sect in Philadelphia.

Forti's 18-year-old son, Joseph, scoffed at the idea that his father's church was an evil, shadowy cult. "They are just like we are. Only they don't believe in smoking and gambling, and they pray a lot," Joseph told reporters. He also claimed that his father often took medicine and had never mentioned anything about faith healing. "I believe whoever murdered dad had a grudge against him or was jealous," he declared.

Sonny Forti, the watchman's 16-year-old son, was the last family member to see Samuel Forti alive. He was with his father until 10 o'clock on the night of the murder.

"Dad wanted me to bring his lunch down to the plant," he said. "He was afraid after that man tried to get in. When I went down, he was joking and laughing. He didn't appear to be nervous. I sat with him in the locker room, and he ate part of his lunch with me. He saved the rest for later. Then I came home."

Could it have been Sonny Forti who took his father's Italian Bible and brought it home? This detail remains unclear. But Sonny did state that he had gone to the foundry every night of the week leading up to the murder, out of concern for his father's safety. Sonny maintained that his father knew that he was in danger. One evening, just days before his death, he came home and asked if any strangers had been lurking about. When Josephine wanted to know why her husband told her not to worry and changed the subject.

THE MAN IN THE HIGH-TOP SHOES

Based upon the statements made by Sonny Forti and foundry employee William Herman, Chief of Police Woffindin concentrated his focus on the man in the high-topped shoes who had tried to persuade Samuel Forti to let him use the telephone. This man, believed Woffindin, had to have been the same tall, thin, middle-aged man who was skulking around the foundry grounds with a flashlight shortly before Forti's death.

Although the dead man's Bible failed to yield any crucial clues, the same could not be said for the rope that had been tied around Forti's neck. Woffindin, who believed that Forti was already dead before he was trussed and hanged, observed that the noose had been tied using a "lock knot," which is used chiefly by sailors. He wondered if the killer might have been in the Navy at one time.

He also wondered about the motive. Killing a man merely because he wanted to leave a religious sect hardly seemed motivation enough to take the risk. Woffindin began to wonder if perhaps there was another woman involved. He began to shift his focus to the love triangle theory. He soon discovered that, shortly before Forti's death, the meeting place of the cult was changed to the home of another member. This change was made because of an undercurrent of jealousy between one of the other cult members and Forti.

Woffindin also learned that Josephine Forti had not been happy that her husband was visiting the home of this cult member several times each week. Samuel Forti's relationship with this female religious zealot had been the cause of several heated arguments.

On Saturday, February 20, Woffindin made a bold announcement: He knew the identity of the killer and promised that an arrest would soon be made.

This, of course, was an old ploy used by law enforcement. If the real culprit was confident that police were following the wrong trail, he might become careless and let down his guard. On the other hand, if the culprit was fearful that the long arm of the law was closing in for the kill, he might get nervous and do something reckless. Most of the time, when a detective says that he knows the identity of a killer, he's merely bluffing to "flush out the game."

So, would Chief of Police Woffindin's gambit work?

THE WIDOW'S PLIGHT

With ten children to look after, Josephine Forti found herself in a dire situation, and her salvation rested not upon the shoulders of Samuel Woffindin, but of a man named T. Duncan Just.

T.D. Just held the position of referee for the state compensation board. In early August, he was slated to hear the case of the watchman's widow. If Forti had died by his own hand, as difficult as that may be to believe, then compensation would be denied. However, if Forti had died while in the performance of his job, she would be allowed to collect benefits. Quite simply, it would all come down to the exact way Forti met his demise.

Woffindin's gambit failed. When the killer failed to tip his hand, the coroner's jury had no alternative but to render an open verdict—meaning that the true nature of Forti's death could not be stated with certainty.

On Thursday, February 25, the coroner's jury met at Norristown, and the proceedings resulted in a butting of heads between local officials. The county prosecutor, Stewart Nase, bashed Woffindin for his tactics, and his unusual theories about secret cults and bizarre love triangles. During the proceedings, Nase declared that he had "washed his hands" of the entire matter.

Woffindin, however, held his ground and insisted that Forti had been murdered. State Police Sergeant Earl Hans and County Detective James G. Gleason, on the other hand, claimed that Forti had taken his own life, though they could not explain how the victim managed to sustain his other injuries.

After ninety heated minutes, the jury rendered its decision. Samuel Forti came to his death by strangulation with a rope in a manner unknown.

For the widow Josephine, this had to have come as a devastating blow, as it did little to help her case with the state compensation board.

On August 19, referee T. Duncan Just declared that it was his fervent belief that Samuel Forti had been murdered, and he called the coroner jury's decision "farcical." But this was cold comfort for Josephine because Just could not find any evidence that Forti had been killed while on the job. If he had been anyplace else but, in the washroom, eating his lunch, just could have awarded the widow compensation. But because Forti was off the clock at the time of his death, it could not be said that he met his demise while in the performance of his duties as a night watchman. Although Just expressed sympathy for the widow's plight and sadness over the whole affair, he declared that he was dutybound to follow the rules.

WOFFINDIN GOES ROGUE

Even though T.D. Just's ruling dealt a harsh blow to the surviving members of the Forti family, it gave Woffindin the encouragement he needed to pursue the matter of bringing the watchman's killer to justice, even if he no longer had the support of the state police and the county prosecutor. Woffindin vowed that he would continue to run down leads, even if he had to go it alone. County officials, however, clung to their opinion that Forti had committed suicide.

By spring of the following year, Woffindin had managed to dig up precious little in the way of any new evidence. On May 3, the watchman's widow appealed the workmen's compensation board ruling, claiming that new evidence supported her claim that her husband had been murdered. According to the petition filed by the widow's attorney, H.I. Fox, one of Forti's sons, had seen boxes stacked beneath a window outside the foundry on the day of the murder, which could have explained how the killer entered the plant. Christopher Torcivia, one of Forti's co-workers, claimed that he had observed an altercation between the watchman and an unknown visitor a week before his death. But, despite the overwhelming evidence against the suicide theory, the official record did not change.

Chief of Police Samuel Woffindin, meanwhile, was bogged down in his problems. He had recently been re-elected to the Montgomery County Police Chiefs' Association as vice president. He was instrumental in spearheading a highly controversial campaign opposing a bill before the State Legislature mandating that police officers provide a suspect an opportunity to obtain legal counsel before being questioned.

One year later, Woffindin was attacked by a violently insane man, and his life was saved when Officer Charles O'Hara fired a canister of tear gas at the assailant. Ironically, Woffindin was forced to resign three years later when the same officer who saved his life brought a charge of intimidation against him. Two of the borough's three police officers resigned in protest, leaving O'Hara as the sole policeman in Lansdale. Although the mayor reinstated Woffindin the following day, the backlog of cases caused the death of Samuel Forti to be forever labeled a mystery.

ABOUT THE AUTHOR

MARLIN BRESSI is the author of *Hairy Men in Caves: True Stories of America's Most Colorful Hermits* (Sunbury Press, 2015) and the creator of the Pennsylvania Oddities blog, which features hundreds of additional true stories similar to those found in this book. He is also the creator of the paranormal website, Journal of the Bizarre.

https://paoddities.blogspot.com

http://www.bizarrejournal.com

www.ingramcontent.com/pod-product-compliance
Lightning Source LLC
Chambersburg PA
CBHW021110090426
42738CB00006B/581